Advance Praise for *A Good Soldier*

"A Good Soldier exposes the pain from a thousand cuts that comes from life with a mentally ill parent. Golden shares in exquisite detail why a maternal mental illness is such an enormous risk factor for children. This shocking, courageous, and compassionate memoir will offer hope to those who feel least deserving of it."

Mitch Prinstein, Ph.D., John Van Seters Distinguished Professor of Psychology, *University of North Carolina at Chapel Hill*

"A brave and unflinching portrayal of the struggle to carve out an authentic life amidst the harsh realities of a parent's mental illness. For anyone trying to grasp an understanding of this particular sort of darkness and its impact on a family, Golden's journey of imperfect survival shines a light on the possibility of resilience and redemption."

Nancy Perlson, LCSW, Board Member, *American Foundation for Suicide Prevention*

"A riveting true account of a young life marred by the mercurial behavior of a mentally unstable parent. A Good Soldier is everything a memoir of this type should be: soul-baring, raw, and compelling, with an added bonus: the prose is pristine."

Leigh Byrne, Amazon Bestselling Author, *Call Me Tuesday*

"Indelibly shaped by her mother's struggles, Ally Golden's perseverance and insight allow her to forge a new life—separate from the shadows of her past—enriched with success, happiness, and love. This timely memoir will give a voice and provide strength to the many who understand this hardship."

Randy P. Auerbach, Ph.D., ABPP, Assistant Professor, Department of Psychiatry, *Harvard Medical School*, Director, Clinical Research, Simches Division of Child and Adolescent Psychiatry, *McLean Hospital*

"A skillfully told, heartbreaking story about growing up and coming of age while emotionally tethered to a mother with severe mental illness. Before you're even finished reading, you want to pick up your sword and help to change the current paradigm of care."

Gina Nikkel, Ph.D., President, *Foundation for Excellence in Mental Health Care*

A Good Soldier

Ally Golden

ISBN: 1540788830
ISBN 13: 9781540788832
Library of Congress Control Number: 2016920308
CreateSpace Independent Publishing Platform
North Charleston, South Carolina

For Mom

Part I

Go, go now, out of the nest, it's time
Circus girl without a safety net
Here, here now, don't cry
You raised your hand for the assignment
Tuck those ribbons under your helmet
Be a good soldier.

—*Tori Amos, "Mother"*

I came into full existence on a humid day in August 1978, on the Robert Moses State Park beach near my grandparents' house on Long Island. I was sitting on a striped blanket with Mom and Dad, a green umbrella overhead and a cooler and boom box nearby. My parents had chosen the infinitely less populated Field 5, and so even though it was a summer Sunday, the crowd on the beach was in a state of controlled chaos.

I wore a yellow one-piece bathing suit with a white turtle on the front. I alternated between dumping pails of sand on my own feet and on Dad's feet. I had a love-hate relationship with sand. It was fun to shovel up and build things with, but I couldn't stand it when it crept up into my bathing suit and made my skin feel prickly.

Beside me, Mom retrieved a bottle of juice from the cooler and handed it to me. I wanted a Popsicle from the ice-cream man instead, but I was too sleepy to argue, so I sipped carefully from the bottle, which was too big for my small fingers.

Planes roared in the cloudless sky. Dad said there was an air show going on at Jones Beach and that he was glad we hadn't decided to go there today. I leaned against Mom, who smelled sweet with sunscreen and felt sticky to my touch. The sunlight made moving pictures behind my closed eyelids, and the low breeze of the ocean played with the tuft of curls on the back of my neck.

"Are you ready for a nap?" Mom asked, squeezing my leg. Mom said she hadn't stopped looking at me since the day I was born, since the day she'd gotten the daughter she'd wanted all her life. Even now that I had been here two and a half years, Mom said she couldn't help touching me, feeling the smooth baby-flesh under her palm. I hoped that would never change, even when my baby sister came in the spring.

I shook my head. "No, Mom, I want to swim."

Dad rolled over on the blanket and gathered Mom into his arms. I loved to watch Mom and Dad hold hands, especially when Mom was wearing her red nail polish. "It's getting a little rough," Mom said.

"Let me take her in, Susan," Dad said. "Just for a little bit."

Mom's sunglasses tipped over her nose as she smeared more sunscreen on my face and small shoulders. "Okay, I guess. But only for a few minutes."

Before Mom could change her mind, Dad and I were running toward the shore, planting our feet over the tiny holes the water made in the sand and avoiding the black and orange shells that were pretty to look at but dangerous to step on. My head against Dad's hairy chest, I rubbed the salt from my eyes and watched Mom back on the beach. She was stretched out on the blanket, her big tummy standing up like a mound of sand, pretending to read *Reader's Digest*. But I could feel her watching, and it made me hold on to Dad tighter.

When our limbs ached with cold and we were struggling to catch our breath, I rode on Dad's shoulders back to the beach. I was so tall I could see the whole world. Some boys in red bathing suits were flying a kite shaped like a scary dragon. And there was an old woman sitting outside an inflatable house, holding a big, colorful bird on her arm. She looked like she was talking to it!

Six girls who looked about the age of my babysitter, Jan, were sunbathing on towels printed with faded cartoons that I didn't recognize. And up in the dunes, seagulls were chirping and nibbling on grass and bits of food that had broken free of the trash bins. Dad dumped me down on the blanket and tickled me until I giggled uncontrollably.

I stopped laughing when I saw that Mom was frowning. I stuck my thumb in my mouth and ran my hand over the edge of a towel, the same motion I used with my blanket, Pinky, at home. "You should have come in sooner," Mom said to Dad. "The current's too strong."

"You're right; I'm sorry. We lost track of time." He grinned at me, and I smiled shyly back. He flipped the boom box, and Fleetwood Mac's "The Chain" floated out of the speakers. "Come on, let's dance." He pulled me up and swung me around, and then Mom wasn't mad anymore. I stretched out like a cat, relishing the way the heat took the drops of water off of my skin, one by one.

"We should get going soon," Dad said. "Traffic on 495 will be ugly."

"Let's eat out Mexican tonight, David, okay? Then we can just get off the Sag and won't have to get back on till the traffic's died down."

He took a bag of Lays out of the cooler and ripped it open. "Sunday's our day to eat home."

"I know," Mom said. "But it's been such a perfect day. I don't want to spoil it by having to cook. Besides, Ally wants tacos for dinner, right?"

I nodded excitedly. "Tacos. Yum!"

Dad smiled. "Well, I guess the Goldens are breaking routine tonight."

Even though there were fun surprises like this once in a while, I liked my family's routine. Things had been different since we'd moved to Washington, DC from Michigan, because Mom didn't have to stay at school all day anymore. On the weekdays, Mom would wake me up in the morning and get me dressed, and then after Dad got ready for work, we would all have cereal together. Then Mom and I would get in the Ford and go to nursery school, and I stayed there while Mom taught at school.

In the afternoon, Mom picked me up, and we went back to our new house in Gaithersburg, a suburb fifteen miles northwest of the city center. Mom filled our home with pretty things like silky drapes and soft, comfy furniture you could sink into. Often, while she was out, she would have picked up something new for the house, and I would help her decide where to put it. Then we would play and read stories, and she would show me all the memorabilia she'd kept from my babyhood until dinnertime. Sometimes, Mom turned on her tape player and recorded me talking about my day so that when I was older, I could remember what I sounded like when I was two.

When Dad turned his keys in the front door, I would stop whatever I was doing and run to meet him, jumping up into his arms and planting wet kisses all over his face. After dinner was my favorite time of day, because Dad would give me a bath with Johnson's Baby Shampoo, pat me dry with a soft towel, and tuck me into bed with my Pinky and stuffed animals.

Sometimes Dad had to go to work on the weekends, and sometimes he went away on one of his trips, but usually we all did something together. This summer we'd gone strawberry picking at Butler's Orchard, when Mom and I wore identical yellow straw hats from JCPenney. We'd also gone to the Montgomery County fair, and Mom had taken me horseback riding once, too. I had been so scared of the huge dappled beast, and the stable boy hadn't wanted to put me on, but Mom said I was big enough. She loved horseback riding, and I would too. They'd see.

"Ugh," Mom said, examining herself critically in the rearview mirror. "My face looks puffy. I'm really putting on way too much weight with this baby."

"Come on, Susan, your body's perfect."

"Sometimes I think you don't see me; that's all."

"Well, I do." He reached over to nuzzle her neck. I could see Mom's face turn pink in the mirror. I let my head drop back against the car seat. I was nearly asleep when I heard Mom whisper to me.

"Next time you'll go swimming with me, won't you, honey?"

I said sleepily, "Let's go back, Mom. Right now."

Born on the cusp of the baby boom, my parents had all of the societal perks of children growing up in the postwar years. They were second-generation Americans, and unlike their grandparents from the old country, they never had to worry about having enough to eat, and coming of age in the transformative '60s, they were encouraged to do—to become—anything they wanted.

My father came from a middle-class Jewish family in Long Island, my mother from an upper-class one in Philadelphia, and their paths converged as undergraduates at University of Pittsburgh in the mid-1960s. My father was a brilliant student who was headed to graduate school in industrial psychology, while Mom was academically lackluster and, like many women of her cohort, was at college mainly to land a husband. On the day she met my father in the university library, my twenty-one-year-old mother was already engaged.

Once Dad came into her life, though, there was no going back. In her mind, he was far and away better looking, more intelligent, and more sophisticated than her fiancé, and the perfect gentleman to bring home to her prickly and overbearing father. She broke off her engagement, and my parents prepared to graduate and marry the following year.

Dad wasn't the settling-down type, especially at that age, but in their day getting married right out of college was the thing to do, and my mother, whose petite cuteness and innocence about life appealed to him, was as good a candidate as any.

They moved to New York City. Mom helped put Dad through graduate school at New York University working as an elementary-school teacher in Manhattan. Though she was objectively successful, getting her master's degree from Hunter College, serving as chapter chairman for the American Federation of Teachers, and teaching on the CBS *National Morning News*, my mother frequently had run-ins with her principals and fellow teachers. Lying in bed at night with my father after the board of education had just forced her to cross a picket line, Mom would lament the injustices of the world, leading him to start calling her the midnight philosopher.

When Dad's birthday was drawn first in the Vietnam draft, they considered moving to Canada. "He'll be killed by his own men," said my mother. Fortunately, he received a deferment to finish his education, and after he received his Ph.D., he convinced Mom to move to Michigan so that he could start a job with a defense contractor. Mom went reluctantly, for Detroit was not exactly the center of Jewish culture, but she picked up teaching where she'd left off and managed to adjust.

But Mom, who'd never made friends easily, was lonely. She felt that Dad didn't pay her enough attention, and she hated the way he read books nonstop during the quality time she tried to organize.

In counseling since her days in New York and prone to crying jags that resulted in multiple therapists instructing my father to hide all the knives and razor blades in the apartment, my mother forcefully articulated her desire to have a baby. After eight years of marriage, Dad finally gave in.

I came into the world three weeks early, in February 1976, via an emergency C-section after nearly twenty-four hours of labor. They named me Allison after one of my mother's favorite third-grade students. I was a good baby—quiet and alert—and both my parents were in love with me from the start. My presence greased the wheels for Dad's announcement that he wanted to get a job with one of the federal intelligence agencies. This would require a move to DC. While Mom resented being dragged around the country while Dad figured out what he wanted to do, she decided that another kid would keep her busy enough.

My sibling was born in January 1979, but it wasn't the sister we'd all been expecting. Neither of my parents was overjoyed. Mom had prayed for another girl, and Dad hadn't wanted a second kid in the first place. My new brother, Andrew, seemed to understand the family dynamic and cried endlessly.

The following winter, my brother was eleven months old, and I was almost four. I sat in the backseat, a sparkly pink tutu covering my small knees. I preferred dirty blue jeans and cotton shirts with decals on the front, and I liked spending my time with two same-aged neighbor boys, Jeremy and Paul. The three of us raced our black and silver *CHiPs* Big Wheels around the block and played *The Dukes of Hazzard* on and underneath Paul's wood deck. But Mom wanted me to act more like a little girl, so I was presently signed up for every preschool dance class that existed.

My brown curls bounced on my shoulders. I could barely see out the window. Droplets of fluffy white snow settled on the glass and slid slowly down, melting at the bottom. In direct contrast to the weather, Christopher Cross's "Sailing" was playing on DC's WAVA station, but only the bass was audible over Andrew.

My cheeks were flushed. I had been rehearsing for a ballet recital for several weeks. The big event was on Saturday. I hoped Dad would finish with business and come to see me, but at least Mom would be there. Too bad Grandma and Poppy lived in New York. Mom would have to send them Polaroids.

I looked at the cars jammed up on the road with big, rounded dark eyes. Mom didn't say anything. She just breathed heavily and tried to shush Andy. The ivory Ford finally broke free of the traffic on 355 and turned onto Montgomery Village Avenue. We rolled over a pothole, and I fell forward. The seatbelt caught me, but Mom instinctively whirled around with her arm outstretched.

"Are you okay, sweetie?" Mom asked.

"Yes, Mom."

"I'm very proud of you, you know that? You're the best dancer in the whole class."

Mom smiled at me, but something in the smile was not there. When I was smaller, Mom's smile took over her entire face. She glowed. I remembered looking up at her from my crib, reaching for the strands of silky hair, the two of us laughing and communicating in our own secret language. Before Andrew was born, Mom was the happiest, loveliest lady in the world. But now Andrew was sad, and so Mom was sad too.

I shivered underneath my puffy Strawberry Shortcake ski coat and mittens. I undid my seatbelt and leaned forward, peering into the car seat. Andy's little face was puckered in a frown. His fat cheeks were red and dotted with tears. He looked at me and let out another loud wail.

"What's the matter, Andy; you don't like the snow?" I said. I turned to Mom. "Maybe he's mad that he's too little to go sledding with me."

"He doesn't know what a sled is yet, honey," Mom said. "Go on; put your seatbelt back on."

Mom drove up the country road that led to our house. Mom and Dad had not planned to move to Maryland at all; they had originally put a deposit on a house in Fairfax County, Virginia. But one day while Dad was at work – intelligence related but in the private sector – Mom had gone out with a realtor and decided to buy this one instead. By the time Dad found out, it was basically a done deal.

The trees, the grass, and the streets were covered with an undisturbed layer of white. Mom pulled into the driveway, the tires grinding on the fresh snow. "Guess I'm going to have to shovel before Dad gets home," she said. She pushed the button to open the garage door and parked the car inside. Mom unbuckled Andy from the car seat and carried him into the house. I trailed behind. I carefully unzipped the Strawberry Shortcake coat and handed it to Mom to hang in the hall closet.

"Can I go play outside later?" I asked.

"Sure," Mom said. "We'll build a snowman. Would you like that?"

I nodded. "Mom? Why does it snow?"

Mom laughed. She put Andy in his singing swing and brushed a few snowflakes from my curls. "Snow's just frozen water from the clouds. It's like rain, except there are ice crystals because the air is so cold. The ice crystals are what make it look white."

"You're smart, Mom," I said. "You should have a job, like Dad."

Mom tickled my belly. "I do have a job, silly. Taking care of you and Andy."

The baby was still crying. I climbed the stairs to my room. I sat down on the carpet and kicked off my shoes. I picked up the Barbie and Skipper dolls that Mom had bought at Toys "R" Us to replace my G.I. Joe action figures. Barbie and Skipper didn't have coats and boots, so I would have to pretend it wasn't snowing next to their house. I lowered the elevator in Barbie's house and escorted the dolls upstairs. After about an hour, my stomach started rumbling. I wanted to watch *Sesame Street* before dinner, so I tucked Barbie and Skipper into their beds and went downstairs.

At the doorway to the living room, I froze. Andy was still in his swing, still crying. But now Mom was crying too. She was sitting on the floor, sobbing into her hands, her whole body shaking. "Mom?" I said.

Mom looked up at me, startled. Her eyes flashed with anger. "Ally, you startled me."

I took a few steps back. "I'm sorry, Mom. Why are you crying?"

Mom rubbed her eyes furiously. "I'm not crying, and it's rude to be nosy."

"What's nosy?"

"Never mind. Just go to your room. I'll call you when dinner's ready." I looked around uncertainly, trying to figure out what I'd done. "What did I just tell you?" Mom bellowed. I turned and ran from the room. I climbed the stairs two at a time and pitched myself onto my bed. I stared out the window until night came and the snow's glow turned the sky orange. Somewhere in the giant, empty house, the baby was still crying.

Mom's mood worsened, and the periods of melancholy became more prolonged, sending her to her bed for days at a time. The only time she got up was when she wanted to "listen." This meant spending hours in her rocking chair with her headphones tuned into old records from the '60s and '70s.

She began seeing a psychiatrist in Washington, DC, and I would go with her to her appointments, sitting in the waiting room with a pile of toys. In this new decade, the country was firmly entrenched in its position as a superpower. The economy was doing well, and we hadn't had a war in a while. We had all the access to good health care that we needed or wanted, and Mom and her doctors were able to experiment with one medication and therapy after another.

Mom wasn't thrilled that so much of Dad's work was secret and that he often had to travel without telling her where he was going. But he was making a good living, so at least we could afford to be members of the Jewish Community Center. Mom loved that there were so many more Jewish people in Washington, DC, than in Michigan, and the JCC exposed Mom to the social contact she craved so desperately. I went to nursery school there, and Mom took me to all sorts of classes and playgroups with other kids my age.

Mom's friendships with other parents didn't seem to stick, though, and so she gradually turned her attention to our neighbors in Gaithersburg. One woman, Darcy, who had a daughter a year older than me, recruited Mom to help her petition the Montgomery County Board of Education to effect a boundary change to allow the kids in our neighborhood to attend a better elementary and junior high school.

After they succeeded, Mom thought she and Darcy would be closer, but Darcy did not include her in the bridge and mahjong groups she formed with other women in the neighborhood. Mom also tried to kindle a relationship with Brianne, a woman who babysat my brother and me while Mom occasionally substitute-taught, but after less than a year, they had a falling out, and we never saw Brianne or her kids again. More often than not, my mother was alone.

For my fourth birthday party, Mom planned a party with a Middle Eastern theme. Wearing a red dress with white tights and patent-leather sandals, I sat at the head of the dining-room table in front of the biggest chocolate cake I'd ever seen. All of my friends from preschool were gathered around me, and piles of colorful presents were stacked by the fireplace. Mom had hung magic carpets on the walls and made candy-filled bottles as favors. My grandfather Poppy, in town from New York, had dressed up as a genie and sat in a circle with the children and granted their wishes.

Mom clapped for the children to pin their wishes on a paper genie that was on the wall next to my growth chart. Mom had drawn the genie herself, and it was pretty good. She blindfolded me first and spun me around. I was so dizzy I couldn't walk at first, so Mom pushed me gently in the right direction. I reached out my wish and stuck it to the wall. "What a wonderful job, birthday girl!" Mom said when she pulled off the blindfold. "That's very, very close."

Dad grinned at me and applauded. The best thing about my birthday was that Dad was home for the whole day, and that Grandma and Poppy were visiting. One by one, my friends tried to pin their wishes on the genie, and the second-to-last person to go, Paul, got his wish right into the genie's bottle. Mom hugged him and gave him a stuffed genie. The group sat back down in a circle, and Mom brought over the presents for me to open. I got some new clothes and puzzles and books and board games, which weren't very exciting, but I almost went crazy with excitement when I opened a toy record player that played real music!

Later that evening, I lay sprawled on the living-room carpet listening to a Supertramp album on my new record player. I didn't understand what "The Logical Song" meant, but it was cool that all the words rhymed. Mom was in the living room with her headphones on, rocking back and forth in her wooden chair. Grandma and Poppy sat on the sofa set watching *20/20* with Dad, who was trying to bounce Andy on his lap while my brother squirmed and threatened to cry. "What a magnificent party," Grandma said. "All of Susan's little touches…it was really special. Did you have a nice time, Davey?"

Davey was my grandparents' nickname for Dad. He hated it, always insisting that people call him David. Not Dave, and definitely not Davey. "Ally had a nice time," Dad said. "That's all that matters to me."

Poppy chuckled. "Davey hates parties; don't you remember that, Joanne? He practically ran away from his own wedding."

"We got married in my father-in-law's backyard," Dad said, handing my brother off to Grandma. The way Dad held him at arm's length, it was like he smelled from a dirty diaper. I'd just seen Mom change him, though. "Can you blame me?" His voice rose a little, and I looked up immediately from my Barbie. I put the toys down and crawled into Dad's lap, my thumb in my mouth.

"Hey," Dad teased. "I thought you said you were going to stop sucking your thumb the day you turned four."

I looked at him for a second and remembered. "Right." I took my thumb out of my mouth and never put it back in again.

"If we'd just had money to contribute," he said to his parents, "we could have gotten married in New York City like real people."

"You had a respectable upbringing," Grandma insisted. "You and your sister had everything you needed."

Dad didn't say anything. Even I knew it was a tired conversation.

"And look at you now," Grandma continued, patting down Andy's spiky hair. He growled at her. "A big house, a beautiful wife and daughter, and now a son too."

"That's what I don't get," Dad said, irritable. He looked out the window and tapped his fingers against his knees. "The second I finally get some traction, the second Susan and I feel like the ground's not going to drop out from underneath us, she goes and gets pregnant."

"Kids are expensive," Poppy agreed dryly. "But you'll manage."

"To hell with managing. I want to learn to fly. I want to see another continent, for God's sake."

"Should have done that stuff while you were living it up in New York City," Poppy said. "You've got a family now."

"Thanks, Dad, I'd forgotten."

"Dad?" I said. "Do you like our house? The lawn's pretty."

Since it was February, it was hardly looking its best then. But I knew it was important to Dad. In the warm months, he was usually outside working in the yard. He seemed to mow the lawn a whole lot, and he was always planting something new out there too, like a small cherry tree or a shrub, dragging a bag of mulch in from the garage and dripping with sweat before he got it in exactly the right place.

Sometimes I would see Dad talking to our next-door neighbor, Linda Gross, over the fence. Dad said that Linda had been a cheerleader for the Washington Redskins just a few years before.

Dad kissed me on the cheek. His lips were moist and tasted like peppermint. "Of course I like our house, sweetie. But someday I'd like to take you to see the apartment where Mom and I lived before you were born. It had a big, long ladder that led up to a little loft. We had our bed up there. It was like a secret hideaway."

"That sounds fun," I said.

"It was."

"Dad?"

"Yes, sweetheart?"

"I'm really glad you're here. Can you stay home tomorrow too?" I would have given anything to wake up and crawl into bed with Dad, his face prickly and his skin warm, smelling like sleep.

"I wish I could, but we've got a lot of new people starting this week. Mom says she's going to paint the nursery. Will you be a big girl and help her?"

"I'm very good at painting," I said seriously.

"You're very good at lots of things," Dad said. "You're a Golden, and Goldens get better with every generation."

Grandma shifted her weight on the couch, and my brother disappeared into her lap. "Your great-grandfather came over from Romania with nothing, Ally. He was only thirteen years old, on a class trip, and he decided to stay in America with only a few coins in his pockets."

"Did he have food?"

"Yes, but not very much. He struggled in this country for a long time. You and your dad and mom are very lucky."

"You make your own luck, Mom," Dad said. "Doesn't just happen."

Poppy stood up painfully. The arthritis in his legs was worsening with age. "Well, that's about it for me. I'm going to bed."

"I don't know what Susan's doing in there," Dad said. "Andy needs his bath."

"Let her relax, Davey," Grandma said. "I'll do it."

"Dad, will you please, please, please read me a story?" I said. I kissed him on the nose. "I have one, two, three, *four* new books."

"One for each year," Dad said. "Sure, Bright Eyes. Go up and get ready for bed, and I'll meet you in your room."

I couldn't remember a happier day. Mom's party, lots of new toys, and Grandma and Poppy, and best of all, the day ending with Dad beside me.

The next year, I went to kindergarten, which was a positive development in my life. I loved to read, and between that and the fact that I was a well-behaved kid, my teachers liked me. I liked going to sleepover parties and play dates and Daisy trips on the weekends, because it kept my mind off how much I missed my dad, who I almost never saw. Mom still took good care of me in those days, making sure my lunchbox was packed and that I never left the house in the bitter cold without Vaseline covering my cheeks. But I always felt like one of Mom's old used toys whenever my brother was around. Andy had stopped crying and started smiling at around a year old, and the more Mom adored him, the more I faded into the background of the household. At least Andy being cute and precocious made Mom happy, because sometimes nothing else could. Dad had stopped trying. I never would.

When I was six, I got a new purple bike, and I spent every day after school riding in slow circles around the cul-de-sac. I was finally getting around all right without the training wheels. The bike had sat in the garage for a while. Dad kept promising to teach me to ride without those embarrassing wheels on the back, but he was away on business trips every weekend.

Then one day before dinner, I took the bike over to my friend Josie's house. Josie's dad taught at the junior high, and he pulled me around on the bike, his large hand on the back of the seat, until I could ride down the street by myself, wobbling and zigzagging but staying upright. Now, though, just a few cruel days after Josie and I had started cruising all over the neighborhood, Josie had the chicken pox and was stuck in bed for a week.

I turned off the cul-de-sac and onto the sidewalk. It was one of the first really pretty days of spring, and I loved the way the purple streamers on my handlebars sparkled in the afternoon sun. I was several blocks away from home when I remembered my tap class. I was supposed to go right inside after the school bus dropped me off, but instead I'd sneaked onto the front porch and grabbed my bike before Mom could see. Now I was going to be late, and Mom would be really mad at me.

I pedaled in the direction of home as fast as I could, and wow, was I flying. I was almost there when I hit a patch of rough concrete and lost control of the bike. I careened into the new bush that our neighbor across the street, Mr. Romano, had proudly planted in front of his mailbox. I scrambled off the bike and stared at the flattened bush in horror.

Mr. Romano was scary. He spent all of his time in his yard, tending to his precious plants, trees, and vegetable garden. He never talked to anyone, not even Mom when she walked by with Andy in his stroller. My heart thudded in my chest. Had Mr. Romano seen?

"What do you think you're doing, young lady?"

I stood beside my bike, paralyzed. Mr. Romano was bounding toward me like an angry bear, glaring at me with his small black eyes. "I...I..."

"You are trespassing on my private property and have ruined my new bush!"

"I'm...I'm sorry, Mr. Romano. It was an accident. I didn't mean to hurt it."

"A bicycle is not a toy," he shouted. "I expect that from now on you'll keep it in the garage until you learn how to ride it. And when I replant this bush, I'd better not see you near it. Now get out of here."

I swallowed hard and nodded. I pushed my bike frantically into my own yard and hid it behind an oak tree in the backyard. I sat down in the grass and cried and cried until I could trust myself to go into the house. Mom was waiting in the foyer. "Ally, where have you been? It's twenty after three."

The lie came easily. "Mrs. Ruez asked me to bring Josie's schoolwork home for her. She's missing the whole unit on Christopher Columbus."

"All right, well, let's go. Just take your dance bag with you. I need to get your brother back home for his nap."

There were still a few hours of daylight left after my tap class, but I did not take my bike out again. I went into my room and shut the door and didn't come out until dinnertime.

A few days went by, then a week. Even when Josie got better, I would not venture out of the house to ride bikes, play hopscotch, or draw on the sidewalk with chalk. On my way to the bus in the mornings,

I scrambled by Mr. Romano's house, terrified that he would see me, and all day at school, I dreaded the moment when I would have to run past his house on my way home.

One Sunday, I stood at my bedroom window, looking down at the street and waiting for Mr. Romano to appear, like a vengeful ghost, in his yard. As if he knew I was watching, he chose that afternoon to replant the bush by the mailbox. I swore I heard him grumbling as he worked, gazing up at my window and threatening me with those small, mean eyes of his. Was he going to come after me?

I had to hide. I pulled down my shade violently and ran for the safety of my closet, where I surrounded myself with stuffed animals and old dance costumes. "I'll never ride my bike ever again," I promised aloud. "Just please leave me alone." I shrank into the shadows until my breathing finally slowed and I fell into an exhausted sleep.

It took my parents a while to notice that I hadn't ridden my bike or played outside in weeks. Finally, one Wednesday evening, a week before the school year ended, Mom knocked on my door. "Honey?" she said. "Honey? Are you in there?"

"I'm here, Mom," I said. I put my Barbie dolls back in their carrying case. "Is dinner ready?"

"Not yet. Josie's on the phone. She wants to know if you have the chicken pox. Now why would she think that?"

"I don't know," I said softly.

"Josie says you won't come out to play. Don't you like her anymore?"

"I like her." I turned away and faced the window. The shade was still drawn.

Mom sat on the floor next to me and stroked my hair. "Sweetie, what's wrong? It's almost summer. You should be outside with your friends, riding that bike Dad picked out for you."

I couldn't take it anymore. I looked into Mom's eyes, so lovely and so concerned, and burst into tears. "Oh, Mom, I did a terrible thing. A terrible, terrible thing." At first I was relieved to be telling Mom about Mr. Romano's bush, but when I was about halfway through the story, I began to feel a little afraid. Because Mom was getting upset again. I could see it in her face.

"And that's why you've been hiding out in your room all these weeks?" Mom said, her voice rising. "You're scared to go outside? That bastard has the nerve to threaten my child?" Her eyes were really flashing now. "You wait here. I'm going to have a little talk with Mr. Romano."

"No, Mom," I said. "Please don't. He might yell at me again."

"Oh, don't worry about that," she said, heading for the door. "When I'm done with him, he won't say anything to you."

I tried to grab Mom's arm, but she was down the stairs and stomping across the lawn before I could stop her. I pulled the shade up and watched at the window as Mom pounded on Mr. Romano's front door with both fists. "Open up! I know you're in there!"

I held my breath and closed my eyes in terror. Mr. Romano was much bigger than Mom. He could hurt her. He could pull Mom into his creepy house by her curly hair just like I'd seen in that Farrah Fawcett movie on TV. I knew Mr. Romano had opened the door, but I couldn't hear him saying anything.

Mom, though, was yelling loud enough for the whole block to hear. "How dare you?" she kept saying. "You've got no one else, so you pick on a little girl? You have nothing to do all day except plant stupid bushes all over this godforsaken place, and you scare a kid to death for a little accident?" I didn't have to look to know that Mom was right up in Mr. Romano's face, spitting the words at her target.

"Let me tell you something. You're lucky she didn't fall and hurt herself on your property, because then I'd be suing your sorry little ass!" This went on for a few more minutes, my eyes growing wider all the time. Mom finally spun on her heel and said, "You owe my daughter an apology." Mr. Romano muttered a reply, and Mom said, "Make it sooner rather than later. Anti-Semite." Then she stomped back across the lawn and slammed the screen door so hard that one of the hinges broke.

She found me in my room. "You have to learn to stand up for yourself," she told me. "People will walk all over you if you let them."

Mr. Romano never actually apologized to me, but he did smile at me and nod when I walked past his house on my way from the bus stop. I was still afraid to ride my bike, but by midsummer, Josie had convinced me to bring it out of early retirement so we could go to the playground on the other side of the subdivision. I never felt quite right living across from Mr. Romano, but I wasn't sure what made me more uneasy: watching the man working quietly in his garden, or seeing the icy looks my mother shot him whenever their paths happened to cross.

Around this time, Mom started getting more involved with her mother, brother, and sister, whom she'd steered clear of for many years. My uncle's family, who lived in Georgia and practiced Judaism strictly, intimidated me, but still I liked playing with my cousins during holiday visits. We went to Philadelphia a few times a year to see my maternal grandmother and my mom's sister and her family.

Although she pursued the relationships, Mom was critical of her family. She complained that her brother and his wife were religious fanatics, that her sister suffered from obsessive-compulsive disorder, and that her mother was a cold fish who insisted on being waited on hand and foot.

Whenever my grandmother and aunts and uncles and cousins were around, I tried to read Mom's cues as to how I should act. If they talked to me, I had to be careful to make sure that my mother was part of the conversation and that she didn't feel left out. It was hard work, and so I was always a little relieved when the visits were over and had passed without major incident.

One late winter day in Philadelphia, my aunt, uncle, and little cousin Ruthie were hanging out at my grandmother's apartment. When my uncle stood up, he accidentally tapped my cousin with his foot. Ruthie didn't react. I, on the other hand, screamed: "Mom! Uncle Terry kicked the baby! He kicked her!"

"Ally," my aunt said gently. "It's not a big deal. She's fine."

"Mom!" I yelled again.

Mom came over, but she wasn't interested in Ruthie. She wanted to visit her father's grave. My aunt's family was leaving and my grandmother said that she wanted to spend some time with the "precious child"—meaning my brother—so my mother and I went alone.

Mom drove fast on the highway. Everything was gray as far as I could see—gray sky, gray pavement. Even the large, dull-green signs with the white writing and the bare trees on the side of the road looked lifeless. There was still a chill in the air too, even though the weatherman on the news said that spring was coming early this year. In the front seat of the car, I huddled into my jacket and watched Mom chew on the side of her hand. She exited the highway and turned onto a narrow, flat street. The road was bumpy and had a lot of holes in it.

"Are you looking forward to starting gymnastics on Monday?" she asked me.

"I hope they have a trampoline." While gymnastics did sound kind of fun, I wasn't looking forward to starting something all the way at the beginning. After two years of ballet, I was just now good enough to do full routines, where I swirled across the stage in glittering, flowing costumes, in time to the music and the movements of the other girls in my group.

But I didn't know a thing about gymnastics, and it was going to be just like when I'd started doing multiplication at the beginning of the second marking period. Math was hard and required me to bite down on my lip and concentrate on each number. I much preferred science class, because we got to play with seeds, and all I had to do was give my clover plant a little water and sunlight, and it would grow.

Second grade was okay overall, but when my teacher was talking and I was bored, I sometimes traveled to a magical land in the sky.

I imagined that I was a warrior princess and Daddy was a king who sat on his plush red throne all day and made important judgments concerning his loyal subjects.

"I doubt you're going to be spending much time on the trampoline," Mom was saying. "You're only taking the first section of this class, and it's meant to give you a foundation in the basics—beam, floor, vault, and bars."

"I can already do three flips in a row on the bar at the playground."

Mom stopped the car by the side of the gravel road. I unbuckled my seatbelt and got out. I trailed behind Mom, who was shuffling into the cemetery, her hands inside the pockets of her fuzzy pink overcoat, her head down. Mom normally didn't shuffle. She walked with her shoulders up, like she was trying to show the world that she was taller than she looked. I ran to catch up.

Mom brushed some dirt off an oval-shaped headstone and knelt next to it. I crouched down too. "This one's your grandfather's."

"What was he like?"

"He was a doctor, but he was quite overweight and smoked like a chimney. There were three of us kids, but he liked me the least. Nothing I did in school or at home was ever good enough for him, and when he would come home from work, my mother would report all my bad behavior in detail. Then, I'd be punished."

I looked at Mom with huge eyes. "How?"

Mom took off her sunglasses and placed them in her bag. "He'd scream at me, call me stupid and lazy, until I'd run away and hide in my bedroom closet and cry for hours."

I felt the torment as though I had been there, and I swallowed a lump in my throat, wishing I could do something to take her pain away. "That's terrible, Mommy."

"My mother insists that he never touched me, but emotional abuse can do just as much damage. My teachers were always sending home poor reports, and I never had many friends, because my father would always criticize them if they came to the house. I grew up alone."

"Why didn't they like you?"

Mom shrugged. "I don't think they loved any of us, really. My brother was my mother's favorite, and my sister my father's. But they'd leave us alone with the maid or at camp for weeks at a time while they traveled all over the world, and they never seemed to miss us all that much. I was the only one who didn't just blindly do what they told me, and that made me their target."

"My father locked me in my bedroom closet sometimes," she went on. "At first I'd scream, but, no one could hear me. I was totally trapped."

I thought about life in our house. I often felt I had to comply with Mom's demands in order to keep the peace, even if they were wrong or didn't make any sense. Like, I was expected to tell my father that he worked too much during breakfast on the day he'd just taken off to spend with us. Or, I should help her persuade Andy, who wasn't even in school yet, that he should have an operation to pin his ears to his head just because they stuck out. "Why didn't you just say yes, so they'd be happy with you?"

Mom considered this. "I don't know, sweetie. I just couldn't."

The wind grew stronger, and a few cold raindrops appeared on the tops of the tombstones. Mom produced a red Totes umbrella and held it over my head. "The only person who showed me any affection was my grandfather, and he died when I was young. I never got over the feeling of hopelessness when they told me I'd never see him again."

At the other end of the cemetery, an older African American girl tugged at the hand of a boy smaller than me. He let go of the balloon he was carrying, and it sailed into the gray sky. The boy began to wail, and the girl slapped him on the bottom. Underneath my feet, the ground began to feel muddy. I felt tears pricking at the sides of my eyelids. Then Mom brushed the dirt off of her overcoat and my jeans, and we walked slowly back to the car.

I felt myself being lulled to sleep by the back-and-forth motion of the windshield wipers. I rested my head against the shoulder belt and closed my eyes. I was startled awake when Mom said, "You're very,

very lucky to have parents who are together and who love you and take such good care of you. I don't want you ever to forget this, Ally."

"I won't, Mom."

"I mean it. Even though your father doesn't always treat us nicely, we are still a family. Sometimes you might feel like things are bad, but they aren't. Okay?"

"Okay."

☙

Mom started substitute teaching in earnest, which was good for everyone because it kept her out of the house, where she had the tendency to sink deeper into despair.

One day when she hadn't worked, I walked into her room, where everything was decorated in heavy gold and maroon brocades, and no light was allowed through the windows. I stared expectantly at the body-sized lump under the bedcovers. "Mom, do we have anything for dinner?"

Without moving, she said: "I don't know. Why don't you look?"

"I can't find anything. Can we go to Giant?"

"Ally, I really don't feel well right now. This has been a very bad day. Bad month. Bad year."

"But I'm hungry!"

Finally, she poked her head out and sighed. "If I leave this room and walk down the hall to yours, what am I going to find?"

"I cleaned!"

"No, you did not. I had the misfortune to open one of your dresser drawers this morning. Do you know what I found?"

"No."

"Well, then let me enlighten you. I found a sandwich. A moldy sandwich, Ally!"

I racked my brain for a plausible excuse but came up with nothing. I had a wooden bedroom set with drawers big enough for Andy to hide in. I didn't have enough clothes to fill them, so they were jammed with all sorts of perishable and nonperishable items. "Sorry."

"You have zero consideration for the house your father and I paid so much money for," she said, sliding off the bed and pacing in front of me. "You have not lifted a finger to help out since you were born. We ask you to keep your room neat, and you can't even manage that. You are spoiled more than that sandwich."

"I cleaned!" I said again.

"I'll go to Giant, but I'm taking Andy," she announced. "You can stay here until every one of those drawers is cleaned out."

At Dad's suggestion, Mom started taking coursework at the local community college, and she found that for the first time in her life, she loved learning. One class in economics particularly excited her. Her professor loved her quick mind and her enthusiasm, and she received an A-plus-plus-plus on a paper about the World Bank that was her pride and joy for months. With our mother working more than she ever had, Andy and I became the stereotypical latchkey kids of the '80s. We'd arrive home from school and fix ourselves a snack of peanut butter and jelly and babysit ourselves for a few hours until Mom got home.

When she was around, we were never sure how the day would transpire. Some days, Mom would fly into a rage at the grocery-store clerk because he wouldn't give her extra cash for writing a larger check, or she would scream, "Why can't all these people just stay home?" at no one in particular when we were stuck in rush-hour traffic. She considered things like having my friends over, helping me sell Girl Scout cookies, and going to my parent/teacher conferences a chore, but then she'd surprise me by doing something nice on my behalf, like hiring a videographer specifically to tape me performing in the gymnastics exhibition.

When I started third grade, Dad started working a little less. At Halloween, I was allowed to have my first party at our house. Dad drove me to the party store and waited patiently at the front while I picked out orange crepe streamers with little black spiders on them and clear balloons that blew up in the shape of ghostly hands.

On the way home, we stopped at Baskin Robbins and bought twenty upside-down ice-cream cones with the faces decorated like jack-o'-lanterns. Andy and I followed the *Highlights for Children* recipe for a witch's brew punch. Andy tried to add one gross-looking ingredient after another, but Dad convinced him that the punch had to be drinkable, and so only a few gross-looking foods would actually make the cut, like clumps of lime-green sherbet, half-frozen red grapes that felt like eyeballs, and masses of thinly sliced, tangled orange peels.

I went back down to our unfinished basement, walking from one end to the other to make sure everything looked perfect. I experimented with having the lights on, and then off, and then on again.

The party didn't start for another hour, but I was already wearing the costume I'd picked out a month ago. I was an angel, and my favorite parts of the costume were the huge pink-and-white wings made of silk and wire. The wings did make it kind of hard to walk around, but as soon as I had seen the model wearing the costume, I knew I had to have it, so I begged Dad, and he bought it for me even though it cost almost thirty dollars. I couldn't stop looking at myself in the mirror on the stairs.

The doorbell rang for the first time, and I ran to my boom box and turned on the tape of haunted-house music. Two friends from school, Christie and Michelle, started a pile of coats in the foyer and clambered downstairs. Christie wore a bumblebee costume her mother had made, and Michelle was a harem girl.

"Gosh, Ally," Michelle said. "Look at all this stuff. This is going to be the best night ever. How long did it take you to make that ice sculpture?"

"I can't believe your mom finally let you have a party here," Christie said.

I glanced nervously at the ice sculpture. Dad had put a towel down under the two-foot-tall ghost, but it was already starting to drip onto the carpet. Mom had never actually said I could put it out, and neat as it looked, I wasn't sure it was worth the risk. I didn't have time to worry about it, though, because lots more kids from my class had come down the stairs, and two of the boys were already hiding in the corners and shouting "Boo!" to anyone who walked by.

I felt overwhelmed by the crowd. Everything I needed to run the party—from the "pin the tail on the black cat" game to my costume competition prizes to extra chips and soda and cups and plates—was stored under the folding table, which was festooned with an orange tablecloth and a giant pumpkin centerpiece. But I seldom had even one classmate over, let alone twenty, and for a minute I wished that Dad would come down and take charge like my friends' parents did when I went to parties at their houses. I'd been looking forward to this party since the beginning of the month, so why now could I not wait for it to end? Why did I feel so alone when half of Mr. Barry's third-grade class had just infiltrated my basement?

One of the girls had brought a Ouija board, and the boys had stopped fooling around with their cups of punch long enough to be intrigued. I was ordered to turn off the lights and the music, so I trotted obediently to the top of the stairs, my wings bumping up against the wall. I was about to flip the light switch when I heard an unfamiliar voice in the kitchen. I peeked around the corner and glimpsed Dad talking to my friend Sarah's mother.

They were sitting at the table drinking cups of coffee, but they didn't seem to be having much fun. Sarah's mom was saying she didn't approve of allowing boys and girls to "congregate" in the basement unsupervised. Dad was nodding and saying that he understood but that he trusted his daughter and could supervise the party just fine from the kitchen. I felt myself getting dizzy. Sarah had told me once that her mother had spent two years in a convent but had then felt a "calling" to have children, so she had gotten married instead of becoming a full nun.

"Ally! Are you coming or not?"

"Ally, turn off the lights!"

But I couldn't move. The voices in the kitchen were getting louder. Dad did not have much patience for other parents. Come to think of it, Dad didn't have much patience at all. But Sarah's mom wasn't about to let up. She wanted him to go down and supervise the party minute by minute, or she was taking her daughter home. Dad didn't seem to care if she did this or not, and this just made Sarah's mom madder. I tugged at the collar of my thin white gown and fought back waves of nausea. My whole party was about to be ruined. Plus, Sarah's mom would hate Dad now and would probably hate me too. Maybe she wouldn't even let Sarah play with me anymore.

More than anything, I just wanted Dad to do something to make Sarah's mom smile. But it turned out the best I could hope for was for the argument to just end. Dad snapped that Sarah's mom could do her kind of parenting in her house, and he would do his kind of parenting in his. He told her when she could come back and pick up Sarah, and then Sarah's mom left—without her daughter.

I walked slowly back downstairs, still feeling like I was about to throw up. I wanted to hurl off the damn wings and throw them out the window. My friends were gathered in a circle. All of the ice-cream-cone jack-o'-lanterns were gone, and I hadn't even gotten to taste one.

"What happened to you?" my friend Jeremy said. "Did your wings get stuck in the doorway?" He and the other boys snickered.

Michelle pointed to a spot on the floor. "Come sit here," she said. "We waited for you. We're playing 'Light as a Feather, Stiff as a Board.'"

"You're going to lift me first," Christie said.

I sat down Indian style. "We have to do the costume contest," I said softly. But the girls were busy getting Christie comfortable in the center of the circle, and no one heard me. Six of the girls gathered around Christie, who had her eyes closed and wasn't moving in the center of the circle. They dug their fingers into her sides, and the group started chanting slowly, "Light as a feather, stiff as a board, light as a feather, stiff as a board." When nothing happened, one of the boys said loudly, "This is stupid. Let's do the Ouija. My sister says those really work."

"Shhh!" the girls hissed.

I imagined Christie floating, floating, floating up to the ceiling and hovering over their heads like a spirit from another realm, her wavy red hair hanging straight down and rippling a little, being so close to the air vents. She floated higher and higher until she bumped up lightly against the ceiling and dropped down a few feet. Then, though, an invisible force threw her upward and smashed her head against the wall! I screamed, "Christie!"

"What?" Christie whispered, annoyed. I opened my eyes. Christie was still on the ground, and the group was still dutifully chanting, "Light as a feather, stiff as a board, light as a feather, stiff as a board."

"Nothing," I murmured. It seemed like we'd been doing this forever. I wished for Dad to come down the stairs and announce that people's parents were here, that the party was over. But the game kept my friends occupied for another fifteen minutes, after which someone finally decided that Christie wasn't going anywhere. Then, I found myself in the middle of a popcorn fight. While the girls squealed around me, with every piece of popcorn that left the bowl I thought about how I'd be cleaning up all night.

Jeremy crawled under the table and picked up the boxed Walkman that I had selected as the prize for the costume contest. "Cool," he said. "Can I have this?"

I shrugged. I just didn't have the energy to yell at everyone to stop throwing popcorn, and I was afraid of what Dad would say when he came down to judge the contest and saw that the world's biggest Jiffy Pop container had just exploded in our basement. "I guess," I said. Jeremy whooped and tore open the box so fast he cut his finger.

"Ow," he moaned. "Get me a Band-Aid, will you, Ally?"

"We don't have any." It may or may not have been the truth, but I wasn't going upstairs. Not until every last kid had left.

That didn't happen for another hour, which was one of the longest of my life. As I waved good-bye to Michelle, my face hurting from smiling so much, I wondered why I'd wanted to have the party in the first place. I untied my angel wings and laid them gently on the floor of the basement closet. I walked back and forth across the floor, listlessly sweeping up the popcorn and untaping the ripped streamers and static-charged balloons from the walls. Dad came downstairs at nine o'clock.

"Is Mom home yet?" I asked.

"Sounded like it was a great party, Bright Eyes. Did you have fun?"

"Yeah," I said automatically. "It was okay." I tried to smile again, but it was too hard this time. Tears pricked at my eyelids.

"We can finish cleaning up tomorrow, you know."

"No, I want to get it done before Mom gets home."

Dad laughed. He sounded almost sad. "I'll go get the vacuum and some towels."

The two of us worked side by side until the basement was back to its preparty condition. Then Dad took my hand and led me upstairs to the kitchen. As he was mixing us some hot chocolate, he said, "You sure have lots of friends. Your dad was always kind of a loner. I'm proud of you."

"I really like Sarah," I said. "And now she's not going to be my friend anymore."

"Why not?" Dad said. "Did you say something about that silly bunny costume of hers?"

"It wasn't that silly. Why did you have to yell at her mom, Dad?"

"Oh, that?" Dad said. He set two steaming cups of cocoa down on the table. Mine was in my favorite snowman mug. "It was no big deal, sweetie. It's just that sometimes adults disagree. I'm sure Sarah's mom has forgotten all about it already."

"I just wanted to have all my friends over for a party," I said softly. "A party at my house, instead of those restaurants Mom's always picking. But it didn't work out. Nothing ever works out."

Dad just looked at me. We sat there for a long time, quiet, just sipping our cocoa.

The year I was nine, I was grounded ten times, one for each year I'd lived and one for better luck. The reasons varied. Whenever I fought with Andy, Mom usually took his side, and I got punished. Sometimes I'd be rude to Mom as a result of this, which would tack on a few extra days of grounding.

Much of my grounding had to do with being "a slob." I couldn't seem to keep my room under control, and Mom and Dad united around this point. I was always writing my parents letters explaining why I shouldn't be grounded for this friend's birthday party, or that school concert. One time I ran away and hid in the woods for a night, which wasn't a good strategy. My parents hadn't even realized how long I'd been gone, and when they did, Mom grounded me again.

One fall afternoon I was standing over Mom, who was on her hands and knees, scouring the bathtub. "Mom, I just cleaned it last week. It looks fine."

Mom looked up at me, her face red with exertion. She was wearing jean culotte shorts, her hair pulled back with a thick purple headband. She cleaned—or wanted someone else to clean—this bathroom often, because it was the only one in the house with a tub. Mom enjoyed soaking, though not in the traditional sense. She didn't stretch out in the dark with scented candles, but rather sat up front, Indian style, splashing herself as the water gushed from the spout. If she took her bath before I went to bed, Mom liked me to sit on the hamper and chat with her while she was bathing.

"I beg to differ," she told me. "It does not look fine. There are brown mold spots in the soap dish."

Steam fogged up the mirror and made my hair stick to the back of my neck. I was supposed to go to chorus rehearsal and was worried I wasn't going to make it. Our director, Mrs. Thompson, would notice that my chair was empty and would give me a demerit. I didn't understand why it was so important to have a spotless house. No one ever came over anyway. Mom didn't like Andy and me having people over, and she didn't have many friends of her own. She seemed to fight with them as much as she fought with me, always slamming the phone down on someone.

Mom took half a can of Ajax disinfectant and dumped it into the tub. She rubbed it around in circles with her brush, making a horrible scraping sound. I took the bottle of Lysol and a sponge from the edge of the shower. "I'll do the sink," I offered. Mom didn't say anything. She just kept pounding away like it was her against the dirt.

"We're both going to be late," she said after a minute.

"Where are you going?" I asked. I rinsed the clean sink off with a cup of water. A few drops of water slid down off the sink and onto the wooden vanity. I held my breath, waiting to see if Mom would notice.

"I have a conference with Andrew's teacher," Mom said. "That woman is incompetent. I may stop by the principal's office to talk about having him switched out of her class. Come in with me while I get dressed."

I followed her out of the bathroom and into the master bedroom. Mom opened the walk-in closet, which was filled to capacity with dozens of colorful suits, blouses, and dresses, not to mention the fifty pairs of shoes waiting patiently on the racks. I leaned against her collection of silk and velvet bathrobes, absently twirling one of the sashes around my finger. "I saw your friend Christie's mother at the gym yesterday," Mom said, struggling into a pink tweed skirt and matching blouse. "I can't get into size sixes anymore? This is going to be a fabulous month."

Dad would be happy. Mom had put on some weight after years of him worrying that she was anorexic. "What did Mrs. Schwartz say?" I asked.

"She mentioned something about Christie taking some other girl to the cabin. Don't you usually go with them?"

"Yeah," I said slowly.

Mom retrieved a satin bra and pantyhose from her underwear drawer. "It's not nice of Christie to invite someone else. Your feelings must be very hurt."

"I don't know how to ski."

"Well, that's certainly not the point. The point is that you're her best friend, and yet she asked this other girl instead of you. Did Christie even tell you she was going to ask Miranda, or whatever her name is?"

"No."

Mom slid her feet into a pair of beige pumps. "It's unforgivable, if you ask me. You've been such a loyal friend to this girl for what, two years? And this is what she does? Well, the apple doesn't fall far from the tree. I always thought the mother was a selfish one."

"I'm not really that mad at her," I said. "I do stuff with other friends too sometimes."

"Well, you should be," Mom said. "It's not right." She rummaged through her antique Chinese jewelry box. "Pick out a pair of earrings for me, okay?"

I stayed in the closet and picked through my mother's heaps of gold, silver, and costume pieces. I hated to see Mom's diamond hoops just stuffed in there with all of the lesser jewelry, so I took them out and cradled them gently in the palm of my hand. I would have given anything to borrow the earrings, but Mom said I was too young and too careless. Across the room, Mom was on the toilet with the bathroom door open. "Come here," she called.

I left the closet and stood awkwardly on the threshold to the bathroom. "What?"

"You are a wonderful girl. I couldn't be luckier to have you as a daughter, and anyone would be just as lucky to have you as a friend. I want you to remember that, and not let people take advantage of you."

"I know, Mom."

"I think you should tell Christie how upset you are that she didn't invite you to the cabin. Maybe when she realizes how inconsiderate she's been, she'll change her mind."

"But I don't want to say anything," I said, looking away as Mom pulled up her pants and flushed the toilet. She stuck her face into the lighted makeup mirror and went quickly to work with a brown eyeliner pencil and rose-colored lipstick.

"Do what you want with Christie, but if you allow yourself to be treated this way now, I don't want to hear you complain about it later."

When Mom finally dropped me off at school, I was twenty minutes late and had missed warm-ups completely. Mrs. Thompson stared at me with cool green eyes as I dropped my backpack in the corner and skulked across the room to my chair in the front row of the soprano section. Even though we were only an elementary-school choir, Mrs. Thompson took her director role very seriously. Only fourth, fifth, and sixth graders could audition, and this year we were singing at both the White House and the Kennedy Center.

The chorus was learning a song from *Flashdance* in four-part harmony and I was under consideration for a solo, but I was only listening to Mrs. Thompson with a tiny part of my mind. Maybe Mom was right about Christie. It was mean of her to invite Miranda to the cabin when I was her best friend. My body shook with anger. Suddenly I couldn't wait for rehearsal to finish so that I could call Christie and give her a piece of my mind. I wished I'd thought about it earlier, when Christie first told me, but I didn't know what to do sometimes. Thank goodness I had Mom.

Midway through elementary school, I gave up both gymnastics and ballet in order to join a kid's bowling league. I was on a team that met every Saturday morning at eight, so Dad and I had to hustle out of the house early, grabbing Burger King breakfast sandwiches on the way. I was unexpectedly good at this random extracurricular hobby and soon progressed to competitions. At my turn, I'd place my feet, clad in some of the smallest professional bowling shoes made, about five feet from the foul line on the smooth, polished wood. My eight-pound ball, customized with the initials "AG," was cradled in my arms. I'd dig my bruised and sore fingers into the holes and wait for the start.

Slowly, but usually more quickly than my coach instructed, I took four steps toward the foul line, my arms and legs moving in sync with the professional bowler's routine. It was as choreographed and painstakingly practiced as any dance routine, yet as ineloquent as a baby's first steps.

Shutting out cheers and taunts from the sidelines, I released the ball with calculated force, my thumb pointing directly toward the center pin. At my size, I could offer the shot minimum power, so any success was all about precision. If I wasn't perfect, the ball would twist rebelliously from the target position, hitting seven pins and leaving three on the left side to pick up on the next shot. I hated being under the gun to get a spare and only managed it a few times a game.

The pressure was all internal, though. My coach wasn't an intense kind of lady, and Mom and Dad were the opposite of those crazy sports parents who get kicked off the bleachers. Dad used my tournaments as a chance to hang out in the used bookstore, and Mom didn't see me bowl once the whole time I competed.

When the commitment to the league involved more than just weekends, I had to stop, because Mom couldn't or wouldn't drive me. I was still in bowling withdrawal when my family sat down to dinner together one Tuesday. This sort of thing had become a rare occurrence. Dad commuted three hours a day to his job in Springfield, Virginia, and when he got home, all he wanted to do was hide out in his den. Mom would insist on his attention, and when he didn't feel like giving it, huge arguments would ensue.

"They just announced more layoffs," Dad said. "I need to start looking for a new job." He looked at the rest of us expectantly.

According to Dad, he was on the verge of losing his job at least twice a year. Since I was little, he'd only switched employers once, and that was his choice—or rather Mom's. She was tired of all the classified assignments and insisted that my father get a normal job. Nevertheless, whenever he threatened the prospect of getting fired or laid off, he wanted the big reaction. "So we won't have money any-more?" Andy said dutifully.

"That's what I'm worried about," said Dad.

Mom ignored him. "I was almost hit head-on by a truck to-day," Mom said. "I thought my life was over right then and there. He slammed on his brakes in the intersection, but just a few more inches…"

"Were the kids in the car?" Dad said.

"No, it was this morning."

I looked at Mom. Her face was almost wistful as she chewed on the side of her hand. Lately, she was becoming more and more obsessed with death. When she and Dad had gone on vacation in Mexico, Mom had had a scare with her scuba equipment, and ever since she had talked nonstop about how she'd almost died in those waters.

Dad spooned most of his serving of Mom's meatloaf into the trash can. Mom's dim smile faded, and I thought she was going to lose it. She hated cooking dinner as it was, and the thought of us not appre-ciating it made her blood boil. I waited. My heart thundered in my chest, anticipating the ugly scene that was bound to start.

"What's going on with school?" Dad asked me. This type of vague question was typical. Dad was pretty clueless. Mom forced him to read the interim reports that the school sent home in the middle of every semester. Sometimes, just to kid around, I asked Dad what grade I was in. He occasionally got the answer wrong, which was funny—sort of.

"Nothing much," I said. "I got an A on my geography test. And I'm thinking about trying out for the talent show."

"And how's chorus?" Dad said.

"Been over since the holiday concert, Dad."

"Oh."

"They're actually making you try out for that talent thing?" Mom said, clearing the dishes from the table. She glared at Dad and snapped on her yellow rubber gloves. "You'd think that after five years at that school, they'd know you can sing."

Andy stood up from his chair and nearly tackled Dad in his chair. Dad wrinkled his nose as Andy slobbered all over it. "Dad! Come see my solar-system diorama! I got an O on it, and Mrs. Perry wants me to bring it back to school so she can put it in the Special Projects case!"

"That's great," Dad said flatly. Andy's face fell, and he allowed his arms around Dad's neck to go limp. I wasn't even mad at my brother for bragging. I just felt sorry for him.

"You won't come see it." It was more of a statement than a question.

"I'll see it later," Dad said. "I'm talking to Ally now."

Andy jumped off his lap and stamped his feet. "You're always talking to her!" he shouted, though that was hardly true either. "You never pay any attention to me. You wish you'd never had me!"

"Andy," Mom soothed. "You know that's silly." But Dad's reaction had set off a temper tantrum, and Andy couldn't be appeased. He wailed at the top of his lungs and managed to summon a few real tears.

"Can you please shut him up?" Dad said to Mom.

Mom glared at him again. "It wouldn't kill you to go look at the damn diorama."

Dad stomped out to the garage, and a few minutes later, we heard a god-awful scream. Dad pounced back into the kitchen. Andy stopped crying abruptly, and the two of us shrank into the corner. He spoke very slowly. "Who. Took. Apart. The. Grill."

"Uh oh," I said.

"I did, Daddy," Andy said, puffing himself up proudly. "But I put it back together. I actually figured out how it worked."

"He did," I said. "It was pretty cool."

"Your son is an engineering genius," Mom said. She couldn't help fussing over my brother, no matter what the circumstances.

Dad looked madder than I'd seen him in a long time, and I thought he might cross that line he'd always managed to avoid. Instinctively, I took a few steps backward. But the blows never came. Instead, he just hollered: "Well, you broke it, of course. Brilliant, as usual. You kids are the laziest, most stupid, worthless brats."

Andy started crying again, and this time I joined him. Mom shrieked, "How dare you? Whatever they are, they are because of you. You're a lousy father."

It happened quickly. Dad moved across the kitchen and pushed Mom, sending her skidding across the floor on her knees. Now everyone in the room was crying except Dad, who slammed the door to the garage and gunned the motor of his Celica. He was gone in a matter of seconds, and a few days later, he moved out.

My parents had been separated for a month when I turned ten. Dad was living in a one-bedroom apartment in Northern Virginia, near his office. Andy and I visited him every other weekend, during which time we ate a lot of McDonalds, got Dad to buy us an endless supply of Garbage Pail Kids cards, and systematically ran through all the activities of his *Things to Do in Washington, DC with Kids* book.

As much of a pain as Andy was, things were better when he was around. When I was alone with Mom, she cried endlessly and hardly left her bed, even when it meant missing important things like my cousin's bat mitzvah. With Dad, I got to hear way too much about how sex with Mom had sucked and that was why their marriage hadn't worked out.

On Dad's side of the family, there was a mass exodus from New York to northern California. When Grandma and Poppy left, I felt like they'd moved to the other side of the world. My brother and I flew to San Francisco over a break from school and had a blast driving down the California coast in Poppy's RV, destination Santa Cruz, Monterey, Los Angeles, Disneyland, Orange County, and San Diego. Grandma held my hand and played with my fingernails as she sang " I Wonder Who's Kissing Her Now," a song from her childhood. As we were falling asleep in the camper, Grandma improvised stories of Tom Sawyer, Huck Finn, and Becky Thatcher. I wished I could stay with her forever.

On Mom's side, people just started disappearing. I saw the mailed envelopes go back and forth between Mom and her relatives and wondered what she said in her letters that made these people never want to see or speak to us again. At one gathering, Mom's aunt gave both my female cousins pretty holiday dresses wrapped in beautiful pink boxes. There was nothing for me, and that was when I realized that whatever they felt for Mom extended to me too.

So we were alone. I started getting Andy up and ready for school every morning, and when we'd come home on the bus, I'd fix us a snack and then a dinner of SpaghettiOs from a can or mac and cheese from a box. At school, we went to a group that the counselor held once a week for kids with parents who were getting divorced. Everyone else seemed mad that their dads were living somewhere else. I didn't mind all that much. I just wanted Mom to meet another man to take care of her, but when I told the counselor that, he said that I was "projecting" my own feelings about wanting to be cared for.

One icy morning I was sleeping over at Christie's house. Christie had an older sister, Candace, and we were playing around on their bunk bed. While I was jumping off, my arm accidentally hit the wood shelf that was nailed to the wall. Candace's precious knickknacks crashed to the floor, and several of them broke.

I gasped. "Oh my God, I'm so sorry!"

Candace was understandably mad, but she was a problem-solving twelve-year-old. "Mom!" she hollered. "I need you to take me to the store to get more Precious Moments. Ally broke mine!"

More surprising was Christie's reaction. "You did that on purpose," she hissed.

I started to cry. "No, I didn't!"

"You did too! I want you to go home now!"

"I'm sorry; I didn't mean it!"

Christie marched to the kitchen and demanded that her mother take me home early. Her mom was confused, but everyone silently moved to the mudroom for coats, scarves, hats, gloves, and boots.

The only one who wasn't quiet was me. I was trying so hard to stifle my sobs that I was hiccupping.

I didn't call Christie all weekend and instead lay in my room. I cried until I was out of tears and then stared numbly at the ceiling. I wondered how many years human beings typically lived. Eighty? Ninety? I was ten. That meant that I had an interminable number left on this earth. My dad was gone, my relatives were gone, and now my best friend was gone. Being awake felt like torture.

Christie really was gone, too. I tried to sit with her at lunch on Monday at school, and she simply picked up her paper sack and walked away. When our friend Michelle asked her what was going on, Christie said that she didn't want to be my friend anymore.

In the counselor's office on Tuesday, Mr. Stark asked me how I was feeling about my dad. "I don't know," I said. "But my best friend hates me, and I want to die."

After demanding the details, he frowned. "I'm going to talk to Christie and her mom. We'll get this sorted out."

I curled up on his couch trying to make my seventy-pound body disappear. Somehow I doubted that.

One afternoon that spring, Mom picked us up from school and drove us to the pediatrician. The doctor's office had a full set of Teenage Mutant Ninja Turtles. Andy always wanted to be Leonardo, so I had to settle for Donatello. Leonardo and Donatello were rescuing a space city some other kids had built out of Legos.

"This city doesn't have a grocery store," I said. "How do people eat?"

"Who cares?" Andy said. "Shredder is going to wreck everything!" As Leonardo, he picked up a Lego man and dropped him into a house with green plastic trees outside. "Take cover, now. We'll save you!"

I leaned up against the toy box at the edge of the waiting room, bored. I was too old to play with Turtles. Besides, I was wrinkling my new denim dress. "Andy, Andy," I chanted. "You're gonna get a sho-ot."

My brother brushed his long bangs out of his eyes furiously. "No, I'm not!"

"Yes, you are. Just ask Mom."

"I'm not going to get a shot, am I?" Andy said warily.

Mom glared at me. "We'll see what the doctor says, but you know the shots are only to give you protection so that you don't get sick."

"I know what they're for," Andy said. "When you get a vaccine, they give you a little dose of the disease so that your body can build up immunity to it."

The purple-haired woman sitting next to Mom was bouncing a fat baby girl on her lap. She laughed. "What a smart boy you are." She turned to Mom. "He is just more precious than words. How old are you, dear?"

"Seven," Andy said proudly.

"Thank you," Mom said, glowing. Next to her, Andy's pale face turned an identical shade of pink. Both of them lowered their eyes and smiled, basking in the attention of the stranger.

I was used to hearing things like this. Just last weekend, my brother had been in the newspaper. He'd dressed up in a frog costume for a play he was in at school, and Dad had taken a picture that won some sort of contest. Even when Andy did bad things, things that would get me in big trouble, people laughed and said he was "cute as a button" and "adorable." It made me want to throw up.

The Woodie's trip last week had been the worst. Out for a day of spring clothes shopping, Andy climbed up on the displays and took the clothes off all the mannequins and put them on himself. I had cowered in the ladies' dressing room, afraid of Mom's reaction, rehearsing what I would say when the anger rained down on me. But nothing happened. A saleswoman discovered Andy first and laughed so hard that the whole store must have heard. She told Mom there was no need to apologize, and that if Andy wanted to try on Woodie's clothes for real, he could enter the summer fashion show that was coming up. Mom was so excited about the fashion show that she didn't even punish Andy.

"Hey, Mom!" Andy said.

"What, sweetie?"

"I made up a great pun. Two silkworms had a race, and they ended up in a tie!"

Mom giggled. She and Andy loved puns. "That's terrific!" She got up from her chair and deposited the paperwork at the front desk. "How long are we going to be waiting?" she asked the pretty African American receptionist.

"The doctor's running a little behind, ma'am."

Mom sighed loudly. "Is there any such thing as a doctor who isn't running behind? I swear they think we have all day to sit here."

"Please be patient, Mrs. Golden. Have a seat, and we'll send you back as soon as we can, okay?"

I chose an orange chair at the end of the long line and took out my library copy of Judy Blume's *Tales of a Fourth-Grade Nothing*. I'd read the same page about eight times when I looked up at Mom. "What am I here for again?"

"The stomach cramps, Ally," Mom said. "We need to find out what's going on. I'm going to see if we can get a referral to a gastroenterologist."

"A what?"

"Gastroenterologists focus on the stomach, the intestines, the bowels, things like that."

Andy laughed. "Bowels. That word's funny."

"I'm fine, Mom."

"I know, sweetie, but you weren't fine when you were doubled over in pain in my bed last week. Don't you remember how much you cried?"

"Does Ally have something wrong with her bowels?" Andy said.

Ignoring him, I answered Mom, "Yeah, but it feels like we were just here."

"Well, you did have that urinary-tract infection. You're just like I was at your age. Lots of little conditions to keep an eye on. Good thing your mother doesn't have to go to an office every day. Who would take you back and forth to all of these appointments?"

"Thank you, Mom," I chorused.

"Do I have something wrong with my bowels too?" Andy asked.

"No, sweetheart," Mom said. "You're just getting your physical for camp."

Andy bounced off the chair. "Yay, camp! Only nine weeks left of school, and then it's summer!"

"How can you hate school so much?" I said. "It's only your second year."

"School's boring. I already know everything."

I rolled my eyes. "Yeah, right, Andy, I'm sure you know everything in the universe."

"Sweetheart, do you still feel like they're not challenging you?" Mom said. "Because I can talk to the principal about getting you into third grade next year."

Andy looked horrified. "No way. All my friends will be in second grade."

"Andy, if you're upset about this, you have to tell me."

"I'm not upset about anything. I'm just bored."

"Well, school shouldn't be boring. Right, Ally?"

"Um…" I said. "Right." I knew how to lie for the greater good.

"I'm not skipping second grade," Andy announced, sitting Indian style on the chair. "And I'm not getting a shot today either."

The purple-haired woman with the fat little girl was called in. She stood the girl up on her chubby legs and held her hand, guiding her to the door. Her eyes still seemed glued to Andy. Mom looked at her watch again. "This is ridiculous," she said, loud enough for the staff to hear. "We've been here almost an hour. These offices really have no consideration for..."

I watched the receptionist's face for any sign of a reaction. Fortunately, there was none. But oh no, wait. Mom was going up to the desk again. "My kids were here before that little girl," she announced.

I glanced around for a place to escape. I could try to scoot back to the bathroom, but that might call more attention to myself. I decided to stand just outside the front door instead, but I could still see what was going on, still hear the voices. I couldn't risk going anywhere else, or Mom would be furious with me for running off.

"Mrs. Lyman's daughter is seeing another doctor."

"Well, maybe you can tell me this. Why does Dr. Marino always have the longest wait? Because I've seen three or four kids come in and out while we've been here. Is there an efficiency problem with Dr. Marino?"

"Would you like to switch, Mrs. Golden? I can schedule an appointment for Ally and Andy tomorrow, and you could come back and see Dr. Lyman or Dr. Goldblum."

I could tell that the woman was losing her patience and that any minute there would be a full-blown argument. I cringed, hoping that if I stood far enough away from Mom, I couldn't be identified as one of her kids. I felt immediately guilty about this. Mom was just trying to get me the medical help I needed, wasn't she?

Andy didn't seem bothered at all. He hovered next to Mom, hip to hip, tapping his foot against the bottom of the reception desk and listening intently. I tried to observe the way he was supporting her. I really should do it the same way, and then maybe she would love me as much as she loved him.

"And wait two hours tomorrow?" Mom said. "Thanks, but no thanks."

"Then I'll ask you again to please have a seat," the receptionist said. "Dr. Marino is in with a seriously ill little boy, but when he's finished I can assure you that your kids will get their checkups."

I thought Mom might leave things alone then, but she just got angrier. "A checkup? Do you know that my daughter was screaming that knives were cutting apart her gut? She needs to see a doctor!"

"Is Ally in pain now?" the woman said. "She doesn't look..." I couldn't watch, but I imagined her clenching her teeth and glaring at the troublemaker's daughter by the door.

Another woman with bright-blue eyes peered through the glass, appearing out of nowhere to save the main receptionist from saying something she would regret to the infamous Susan Golden. "Ally, why don't you come on back? We'll find you a room, and you can get changed into a gown."

"We'll all come back," Mom corrected. "Once I get that doctor's attention, I'm not letting him out of my sight."

So we all trooped out of the waiting room, through the maze of brightly painted halls with a different medical contraption on every corner. I smelled antiseptic, heard the muffled sound of a child's cry from behind a closed door. Andy must have heard the crying too, because at that moment he started whimpering that he'd just wait outside, that he really didn't need to get any shots today.

When Dr. Marino finally showed up and casually mentioned to Andy that he was going to give him a "booster" of some kind, my brother totally lost it. I was certain you could hear the screaming through the entire medical building.

"I don't feel well," I said to Mom in the midst of the chaos of a nurse trying to hold a squirming, crying Andy down on the examining table. "I'm going to wait in the car."

"Are you kidding?" Mom said. "You're sick, and you're in a doctor's office, and you want to wait in the car? Andrew's going to get this goddamned shot, and then you're going to tell Dr. Marino what's wrong with you, and I don't want to hear another goddamned word about it."

I never got a formal diagnosis for my occasional episodes of horrible stomach pain, but Mom had a copy of *The Physicians' Desk Reference* and said that I had something called irritable bowel syndrome. She found out about a monthly support group led by her gastroenterologist and signed me up. At ten, I was the youngest person in the discussion circle by thirty years. Mom often accompanied me, prompting me to speak up so that the other attendees could "hear how articulate I was."

Meanwhile, Andy and I were shipped off to camp for another summer. We went to a different place every year, most of the time through the Gaithersburg Park District. These camps grouped kids by grade, and your "tribe" was led by a sixteen-year-old high-school kid. The themes varied. At sports camp, you did a different game or sport every hour out in the hot sun with the weeds tickling your exposed legs and gnats flying into your nose and ears. I wasn't a fan of that one and counted the hours until I could go home. It didn't occur to me to tell Mom I didn't like it, though. More or less, I did what she told me to do.

At a more general day camp housed at my future high school, there were red barrels full of "bug juice" (Kool-Aid), penny carnivals, bus trips to Chuck E. Cheese's and the Washington Children's Museum, and inappropriately scary movies on rainy days. At theater camp, you were shut up in an air-conditioned school building making costumes for the play your group was putting on at the end of the summer. There, I learned the essential skill of making clothes out of cardboard.

In the summer of 1986, though, Andy and I went to a camp called Seneca Creek, which was the real deal and was later the site of the terrifying 1999 movie, *The Blair Witch Project.* I learned to kayak, ride a horse, shoot a bow and arrow, properly swim the crawl, do a double flip on the trampoline, and make a friendship lanyard with ten different colors.

We slept in a tent on top of the massive Hamburger Hill, which was haunted for sure. My new friends and I linked arms and strolled through the well-appointed grounds singing Tears for Fears' "Shout" and the soundtrack to *Top Gun* at the top of our lungs. We carried ratty, blue duffel bags crammed full of wet bathing suits and towels and French-braided each other's hair with lice-infested hair ties. Every day, as the bus pulled away from my house and headed off to another new adventure at Seneca Creek, I was able to believe that the life of a kid was actually supposed to be fun.

At the end of the summer, Andy and I flew back to our grandparents in California. By then, Grandma had started taking care of our cousin Lisa. Mom talked constantly about how she'd replaced her grandchildren, who were older and therefore uninteresting to Grandma, with this new toddler. Andy and I accepted this as truth, and when we arrived at our grandparents' house in the East Bay, we actively resented Lisa's presence and jealously sought the adults' attention in any way we could.

When we returned home, we found that after less than a year of living in Virginia, Dad had moved back into the house. Before Andy and I started school, Mom insisted that the four of us go to Virginia Beach in the middle of a hurricane. The car almost blew off the highway and we spent most of the trip at the movie theater.

I didn't question why my parents, who clearly didn't get along and may or may not have loved each other at all at that point, would make the decision to get back together. All I cared about was having another adult in the house again. By this time, Mom was seeing her DC psychiatrist, Aaron, several times a week and had an identified illness known as major depression. She was going on a new medication that they were sure would cure her. I thought that Dad's presence—scattered as it still was—would put a greater distance between me and "the illness." I was wrong.

One afternoon in fifth grade, I waited and waited outside the school building. It was a quarter past five, a good half hour after my chorus rehearsal had ended. The school grounds, even the teacher parking lots, were empty. I tapped my foot against the concrete and watched every car driving past for a sign of my mother's navy Subaru. Nothing.

I wished I had taken Christie's mom up on her offer to drive me home, as Christie had recently decided she was willing to be my friend again. We were closer than ever now, reading Shel Silverstein poems aloud to each other in silly voices, secretly trying on makeup in the bathroom at school, and sharing huge boxes of Milk Duds at the movies.

Mom had said she was coming. I felt stupid. How many times did I have to be left stranded outside before I realized that I should take any ride I could get?

I tried to distract myself with thoughts of school. It was nearly Valentine's Day, and the fifth and sixth grades were having a dance in the cafeteria. Maybe I should think about liking Tony Caruso. At Michelle's sleepover, Christie had whispered that Tony wanted to ask me to the dance but thought I would say no. Tony wasn't bad looking. A little gangly, maybe, but cute enough, with spiky blond hair, blue eyes, and round-rimmed glasses.

The sun was going down already. Mom wasn't usually *this* late. I walked back inside the school and dialed my home number on the pay phone. No answer. I figured I might as well get going—it was three miles home. I cut across the athletic fields and headed down Stedwick Road. Cars stuck in rush-hour traffic were jammed at every intersection, blinking their lights and honking irritably.

My head throbbed with anger. I worked hard. I got good grades. I never broke any rules. My parents didn't have to pry me off the couch so I'd get involved at school. And yet here I was. I walked past Burger King, and my stomach rumbled. I'd have given anything for a Whopper Supreme and fries right then, but Mom would have been pissed if I had spoiled my appetite for a frozen tuna-noodle casserole. By the time I turned my key in the front door, the streetlights were on. I walked inside and dropped my backpack over the banister. I almost tripped over my brother, sitting in the hall with his arms draped over his knees.

"Shit, A," I said. "You scared me."

"Hi," he said in a small voice. "Where were you?"

"Mom was supposed to pick me up," I snapped. "I had to walk."

"Ally?" Andy said. "Mom's really sick. I think you better come upstairs."

I turned on the hall light and saw that my brother had been crying. I softened. "I'm sure everything's okay. She probably just has a migraine."

I found Mom facedown on the king-sized bed in a T-shirt and underwear. It looked like she hadn't gotten dressed that morning. "Mom?" I said, stepping closer to the bed as Andy hung back. "What's wrong?"

Mom turned over in the twisted blankets with effort. Her face looked washed out, and her eyes were red-rimmed from what looked like hours of crying. "I can't handle any more, Ace. I just can't."

"Any more of what?"

"Your father's not coming home again this weekend."

I sat down and patted Mom's sweaty back. "That's all right, Mom. We can do a girls' day at the mall."

Mom didn't seem to hear me. She stared at the wall, blinking only about once a minute. "He didn't really want to get back together. And we haven't had sex in months. He doesn't love me anymore."

"That's not true, Mom," said my eight-year-old brother.

She sighed. "Yes, it is. I just haven't wanted to see it. I can't really blame him. His parents never wanted him to marry me, you know. They were thrilled when we separated. And now they think I'm a terrible wife and a terrible mother to you kids."

The guilt from being mad at Mom for not picking me up grew like a poison balloon in my stomach. "You're a wonderful mother," I said firmly. "You take care of all of us."

Mom produced a bottle of pills from behind a hunter-green pillow sham. "I would have been gone already, but I had to see my children one last time." At that, Andy ran from the room. He knew what Mom meant by being gone.

My eyes darted frantically from my mother to the phone on the bedside table. What was I going to do? "What happened this morning, Mom? What happened to make you so upset?"

"Nothing," Mom said. "I just can't do it anymore. I'm sorry, Ace; I've tried, but I'm just one of those people who never should have been here, you know? I've had forty-one miserable years. You don't want me to be miserable anymore, do you?"

"You're not miserable all the time. You have fun. We have fun together." But Mom was crying again, and my panic was growing. I started crying too. "Mom, please don't hurt yourself. We love you so much. We need you."

She fell back down on the bed then, as if her ninety-five-pound frame was too heavy to hold up. "It's what has stopped me all these years. I don't want to leave you and your brother without a mother. But I'm no good to you like this."

I looked in the dresser mirror, hating the sight of my windblown hair and flushed face. "Yes, you are. We can make things better. I'll talk to Dad for you, okay? We'll go to the beach this summer, and we'll spend a whole week. I know Andy and I haven't been so good lately. I'll be better; I promise." I lay down next to Mom and hung on as if I could persuade my mother back to life just by clinging to her. I felt like I was in a car teetering on the edge of a cliff, pushing my weight to the back as it swayed back and forth, back and forth.

"I don't know, Ally; do you think it's even worth it?"

"Of course it is."

Mom rubbed her eyes with small, balled fists. "Well, I'll try—for you. But if you find me in here tomorrow, and this Vicodin bottle is empty, please don't hate me. I just don't know if I'm strong enough."

"Mama, don't you have an appointment with Aaron this week?"

"Aaron's away...again. But someone's covering for him. Maybe I'll go."

I tried to smile. "Good. I'll drive down there with you." I stood up. "I'll go make a salad to go with the casserole. Are you going to be okay while I'm gone?"

"I guess so," she said, covering her eyes. "I'm just going to sit here awhile."

I left the room but did not close the door. If I was honest with myself, Mom and I hadn't been getting along at all lately. I'd started calling her Susan, mainly just to tease, but it was still disrespectful.

Last week, when we'd been in the car with Christie, Mom had gotten my friend to admit that she never talked back to her mother the way I did to mine. And it wasn't right. Because Mom always wanted to talk when something was upsetting me.

Sometimes she did really nice things too. Like the previous month, when a neighbor had asked me to babysit, and Mom said she didn't think it was a good idea because one of the kids had epilepsy. What if the child had a seizure while I was alone with her? I wasn't even eleven yet—I'd be so scared.

Not all mothers would think about this, but mine did.

This was what made it tricky.

I wondered if somehow, she could go back to being the mother she was before my brother was born. I knew that Mom was in there, and a part of me thought that maybe she could come back—as long as she was alive and I loved her.

I thought about my behavior over the last few months and concluded that I was the most rotten kid in the world.

Andy eased out of his room. "Is Mom going to die?"

"I hope not, A. I think she'll be okay tonight, but you're going to have to be really good from now on. We have to show her we love her."

Then Andrew was glaring at me, looking like a miniature version of Mom when she was angry. "You're one to talk. If she hurts herself, it'll be your fault, not mine."

"It wouldn't be either of our faults," I said. But I wasn't so sure.

Later, Mom told me that my love was what had saved her. I'd obviously made the correct moves, so I tried to remember what combination of words and actions I'd used to keep her alive in case it happened again. And once I was sure I had it down, I felt my power grow.

In the spring, Christie told me her family was moving to Honduras. Her dad worked for the US State Department, and he'd be stationed there for the next two years. It was unclear if they would ever move back to the DC area.

Losing friends this way was not an uncommon scenario for me. Due to the temporary nature of government employment, families moved in and out of our community all the time. But with Christie, it felt different. I had gotten my best friend back only to lose her again. In the month before Christie left, I probably cried more days than I didn't. We spent every spare moment together, going to the mall dressed as twins and picking out cool stationary to write letters to each other on. Mom seemed sad for me and even let me stay home from school so I could go with Christie and her family to the airport. When she left, I thought the emptiness would swallow me, but I kept going to school and singing in chorus, and life was the same, except every day I'd rush home to check the mailbox for a letter from Christie.

Sixth grade arrived. It was the end of my elementary school tenure and my class ruled the place. I was the captain of the patrol squad and vice president of student government. I was my school's representative in the Montgomery County Honors Choir, and I won the county superintendent's writing competition. I had become a consummate high achiever, which my father could relate to. He now had a two-seater Toyota MR2, and we would ride around with the windows open, regardless of how cold it was. Dad liked Rod Stewart and especially the song "Forever Young," which he said reminded him of our relationship. I wasn't convinced that Dad wanted me to remain forever young at all, but it was a nice sentiment.

And most importantly, for the first time in my life, I was popular. My new friend Grace, the kind of person who'd been popular all her life, had moved to Gaithersburg and immediately started a club that all the girls wanted to be in. She chose me as her secretary, and my life was forever changed.

Until junior high, that is. We had barely decorated our new lockers at school when Grace announced that we spent too much time together. She thought that being so clingy wasn't good for me and that

I needed to have other friends, which really meant that *she* needed to have other friends. I found myself on the outside, with only a few people to eat with at lunch and go out with on the weekends. I had a crush on a boy I had no chance with because I was a nerd, and the eighth-grade boys liked to torment me because Mom had apparently almost run one of them down with her car.

I wanted to have a bat mitzvah because I thought it would be a chance to have a cool party at a hotel and invite all the kids I wanted to be friends with, so I started going to Hebrew school and learned all the material for the ceremony in six months instead of two years. But what was supposed to be one of the most significant events in my life ended up being a huge disappointment.

Dad, who wasn't into Judaism, thought the whole thing was a waste of time and only concerned himself with whom he should and shouldn't invite from his office. Mom took charge of every-thing, creating her own dream party without even asking me what I wanted. I didn't think I could protest the invitations—staid Japanese flowers—or the music choices—easy listening. But when Mom took too much time getting ready and made me late for my own ceremony, I couldn't give in anymore. I burst into tears and cried hysterically until she finally got in the car and sped all the way to the hotel. I dried my eyes in the bathroom, got up on the stage next to the rabbi, and smiled at my guests before chanting my Torah portion in flawless Hebrew, but I was mad at Mom long after it was all over.

That year I developed a hell of a temper. Mom would say some-thing to set me off, usually about my weight, which was too high, or my personality, which was too dour, and next thing I knew, I'd be pac-ing around her bedroom, screaming until I was hoarse. I slammed doors so hard that two of them got knocked off their hinges. After one of those fights, Mom would give me the silent treatment for a few days, and she relished how it made me squirm with remorse. But the guilt I felt after I'd calmed down wasn't enough to stop the rage from coming back again and again and again.

I'd just turned fourteen the night she came into my room without knocking and sat down Indian style on my bed. "I have something to say to you," she said.

I was working on a paper for English in which I wasn't allowed to use the letter E. "I'm busy," I said.

"You're always busy. Well, I'll tell you, when I'm gone, you can sit on your damn computer all you want."

"Fine," I said, sighing. "What?"

"I just want to tell you that you are systematically destroying our relationship every day with this behavior of yours."

I looked at her and noticed she had on yet another new bathrobe. Mom had acquired a pretty bad catalog-shopping habit. Her room was filled with half-open cardboard boxes, and another half dozen of them, which had arrived in the last week, were still sitting in the foyer. She'd also started taking her prescription drugs around the clock for her headaches. She substitute-taught only a few days a month now, and usually, when I came home from school, she was asleep in bed with the TV on.

"What do you want me to do?" I said sarcastically. "Flunk out of school? I don't get it. I get straight As. I don't drink or smoke. I don't break my curfew...ever. I'm freaking perfect. But it's not enough for you."

"It's that attitude that I'm talking about. Everyone keeps telling me you're being a teenager, even though you've been this way since the day you turned ten."

"What about your attitude?" I said. "Oh, I'm sorry; I forgot; you're allowed to act any way you want."

"That's right. It's my house. I'm not really surprised that you're the way you are. You're just like your father. Too serious—all your father did on our honeymoon was read, read, read—no sense of humor whatsoever, and abusive." She paused thoughtfully. "I don't know where you got to be such a slob, though."

"If you hate Dad so much, why'd you get back together?"

"I ask myself that every day."

I glared at her. "I wish he would leave again and take me with him."

Her eyes glittered with an anger that was so intense it was almost hate. Usually I feared this look, but tonight I just stared back at her and tried for the same level of intensity. "Funny how he's the good guy, even though he's never here and never talks to you and never solves your problems or takes care of you when you're sick," she snarled. "I'm the only real parent you have. Who picks you up from the bus stop when it's raining? Certainly not him."

"Not you either," I shot back. "That was one time, and it was, like, six years ago! Dad has to work. I get it."

"You get it," Mom mimicked.

"What the hell do you want?"

"I want you to act like a human being."

"And I want you to stop saying what a shitty kid I am all the time. A shitty kid wouldn't cry and beg you not to kill yourself. A shitty kid wouldn't give a damn."

"I am not going to apologize for my illness," she said. "If you can't support me unconditionally, then I suggest you don't bother!"

"Maybe I won't."

"You know, you could really learn something from Andrew. We get along beautifully."

"Yeah, whatever," I said. "You're going to love him more no matter what I do."

She ignored me. "I can see Andrew and me having a close relationship for the rest of our lives. As for you and me, well, like I said before..."

"Would it be remotely possible for you to leave me alone?" My head was really pounding now. I didn't even want to finish my paper anymore. I just wanted to sleep.

"No, I don't think so."

"Please?"

My mother kept going. "You are such a little bitch," she said. "No wonder you don't have any friends."

"Get out!" I screamed. "I hate you!"

"No," she said, standing over me and glaring. "This is my house. If anyone's getting out, it's you. How dare you treat me like someone off the street?"

"I don't treat people on the street like this!" I said. "They aren't psychopaths!"

She said something else, but I was having trouble hearing. Her voice was going in and out like bad phone reception. I closed my eyes for a moment, and when I opened them again, I heard her clearly say that no one would ever love me and that I deserved to be alone for the rest of my life.

The fire that had been burning softly in a small corner of my belly suddenly raged upward and swept through my entire body, propelling me forward. I staggered up from the desk and just started hitting her. I let her go when Andy came charging out of his room and yelled at me to stop. I slowly released my hands and just stood there, shaking, not believing what I had just done.

High school was kinder to me than junior high had been. I was the objective definition of popular—not in the cool crowd by any means but friends with a lot of different people. I loved being around my friends and their parents, although I couldn't help feeling this vague sense of alienation, like there was something that set me apart, that I didn't really belong there. I resented how involved my friends' moms were in their lives, and I often chided myself for being jealous.

Occasionally, when I was over at someone's house, I would sit at the kitchen table quietly, just watching and listening. My friends' parents would try to get to know me, asking me questions about school and my own family. I chatted about the first topic eagerly and longed to talk about the second, but I was too ashamed.

I kept my straight-A record all through ninth grade, but at the beginning of tenth, I found myself in danger of losing it due to the dreaded mile run in gym. Girls had to run it in under nine minutes in order to get an A.

The day of the race, I was terrified. I stood on the grass outside the metal gate that led to the track, staring at my unforgiving gym teacher's stopwatch. She shouted "Start!" before I was ready, and I pictured the numbers on the watch flying forward. I leapt into the center lane. My throat was raw as I gulped in frigid fall air, and the cramp in my gut was whining for mercy. My classmates and I were like a pack of horses, exactly alike in our regulation T-shirts and sweats, our sneakers pounding the pavement like rolling thunder. I wiped frantically at the stray hairs plastered to my face, squinting in the sunlight, chest heaving.

After a half mile, I gave in to the temptation to walk for a few seconds, which was like having a near-death experience and being forced to go back. A girl I didn't recognize came up beside me. "You have to keep going," she said. "You're the only thing that's motivating me." We took off again together and finished in just under eight minutes and thirty seconds.

Her name was Tina. She had just moved to Maryland from New York, and she became my best friend.

By the time Tina and I were both cast in the spring musical, *Little Shop of Horrors*, I was a force to be reckoned with in the drama department. I was one of the only kids to be cast in every show since I'd started high school. Between theater, keeping up my grades, and going to parties on the weekends, I was hardly ever home. I left the house before seven and didn't get back until around eight, falling asleep in my books while trying to get my homework done in the precious hours before midnight.

Then, at the end of tenth grade, my scoliosis, a curvature of the spine I'd first been diagnosed with in seventh grade, started to get worse. The curve was in the base of my spine, too low for the corrective brace usually associated with scoliosis treatment. Mom whisked me off to an orthopedist, who said that while my condition didn't require immediate surgery, it might cause future problems. There was also the possibility that it would cause a loss of height, and I was already pretty small.

Mom, of course, took all this to mean I should have the operation as soon as school got out for the summer.

I didn't question Mom's judgment about this, and neither did my father—until I caught pneumonia in the ICU. They'd broken several of my ribs in order to reconstruct my spine, and both of my lungs had collapsed. I was in and out of consciousness for several days and in enough pain to require a constant morphine drip, but I was aware of my parents arguing over my bed, aware of hearing my father cry for the first time, aware of him clasping my cold hand and saying over and over, "What have we done?"

My recovery was supposed to be three to six months, and I was ambivalent about how long I actually wanted it to take. On the one hand, Mom relished the opportunity to take care of me when I couldn't move around or do much of anything by myself, and she was kind and gentle in a way that almost made me not want to get better. She told everyone who would listen how strong and brave I'd been through the whole thing. And Dad was making an extra effort to spend time with me, driving me to Georgetown for dinner and a new wardrobe as soon as I could walk.

But there was the issue of school. The doctor had advised me against going back in September, but I was going to start on time if it killed me. I didn't want to be behind. On the first day of junior year, I showed up wearing a giant plastic brace under a bulky sweater, on minimum medication so that I wouldn't space out in class. And when our principal stopped me in the hall and said he was proud of me, for a minute the entire ordeal felt worth it.

A few weeks into the semester, Tina and I went to a soccer game at Rockville High School to meet Kevin, one of my online friends from the summer, in person. Kevin introduced us to his teammate Jack, who must have found the boxy look appealing, because he asked me to his homecoming dance. That night in late October was the first time I'd been out of my equipment in more than four months, and Jack was very careful with me. He guided me around protectively and touched the pale skin on my back like I would break if he applied too much pressure.

Jack was the first guy I kissed and actually kept seeing afterward. We hung out with each other all the time during our junior year, and one afternoon, we sat at my circular kitchen table, eating out of a bag of Oreos. Mariah Carey bombarded us with her incredible vocal range from upstairs in Andy's room, the drum beat of the song vibrating against the walls. I slid off my plain white Keds and let them drop to the floor. Jack grabbed my left foot under the table.

"I so shouldn't be eating these," I said, lazily licking the cream filling off a cookie and raising it to my mouth.

"Oh, come on," Jack said. "What did you have for lunch, like, one piece of lettuce?"

I playfully slapped him on the arm. "You make me sound like an anorexic." I pulled my hair into a ponytail and stood, stretching my arms behind my back. In the congested fridge, I found a half-empty carton of milk, and after sniffing it gingerly, I poured two glasses.

I grabbed my metallic gold backpack from under the table. "Fun's over. It's SAT prep time for you."

Jack wrinkled his nose. "Why did I ask you to help me again?"

"Because you really want to get that eleven hundred," I said.

"Do I? I'm not going to some big-shot college like you."

"Fine, be a slacker. See if I care."

"Okay, okay. But only if we can go see *A Few Good Men* after dinner."

"Can't," I said. "Rehearsal." I looked around nervously. "I hope Mom's going to drive me." Things had pretty much reverted to the status quo since I'd gone back to school, and I was always worried that Mom wouldn't be around—or would simply refuse—to take me where I needed to go. I couldn't wait to get my driver's license after the New Year.

"Where's your mom?" Jack asked, reading my mind.

"I don't know," I said. "She subbed in Germantown today, I think. I really need this play to be over. I haven't studied for midterms at all."

My eyes traveled around the kitchen, which, though unblemished by dirt or grime of any sort, was in its usual state of controlled chaos. Giant Food circulars, pale-blue coupon envelopes, and unopened credit-card applications overflowed from the countertop, and different versions of Andy's school picture were taped precariously on the wall above it. My lightly pimpled, thirteen-year-old brother looked alternatively sweet, smug, and smoldering, and older than me in all of the pictures. Mom had written a list of family chores in purple ink on the whiteboard, which had been erased so many times it looked blotchy. My eyes stopped on the list:

Andy:

- Defrost meatloaf
- Make dentist appointment
- Collect recycling and put in garage
- Brush Magic

Ally:

- Clean bedroom closet
- Vacuum family room
- Clean upstairs bathroom
- Return call from Driver's Ed

But hold on. There was something, a strange object, hanging on the right side of the whiteboard, next to my list of chores. It was oval shaped, white, covered mostly in blackish-red...what the hell? No, it couldn't be. There was no way. I shook my head from side to side. This had to be a dream.

On the other side of the table, Jack followed my gaze. "Holy shit," he said, when he realized what he was looking at.

Seconds later, I was still trying to comprehend it. The furnace crackled on, igniting the still air, doing what it was supposed to. I didn't feel my heart beat for a long time. "No..."

My mother appeared in the kitchen then, standing next to the whiteboard as if giving a formal presentation. I hadn't heard her come down the stairs. She must have floated, like an apparition. "Hi, Mrs. Golden," Jack said awkwardly. "We didn't know you were home."

"Hello, Jack."

Somewhere in my brain, thoughts were racing along, neurons firing, making connections. How could Mom be home when her car wasn't in the garage? Why was she wearing a hat that matched her sea-green suit and pumps, like something out of the 1960s? What could make her, a human being who gave birth, slept at night, brushed her teeth, what could drive her to make a conscious decision to tape a soiled menstrual pad to the whiteboard in the kitchen, for the boy her daughter was dating to see?

Mostly, though, I was just numb.

"I thought a little visual demonstration might get your attention," she said. "Since you've ignored one chore in particular for the last two weeks." I searched her face for the typical signs of rage, but I found none. Her eyes were cool, soft. She looked almost pleased with herself.

"Mom...where?" They were the only words I could utter, and my voice was low and husky, like someone else's.

"She asks me where," my mother said, smiling at Jack. "Where indeed. You've lived in filth for so long that you don't even notice anymore, do you? You think no one lives in this house but you. You leave your stinking, bloody mess on the floor for all of us to sample. You—"

"Mrs. Golden," Jack said. "I think that—"

"I know what you think. You think she's hot stuff. You think she's got something to give you. Well, now you can see for yourself."

More static filled my head. What was she doing in my bathroom? How did it get on the floor? Did our cat, Magic, pull it out of the trash basket? Or did my mother purposely reach in and pull it out herself?

Why would she do it? What had I done now? The questions came faster and faster until I couldn't make them out anymore. My body began to shake, and my eyes flooded with tears.

I couldn't look at Jack. I couldn't look at him ever again.

"Please take it down," Jack said, his firm voice coming from another world.

"Oh, I think we'll leave that job for Ally," my mother said. "I'm late."

Something was burning. I felt movement in my toes. It traveled up through my legs and my torso. I broke free, propelling myself out of my chair. I ran, choking and sobbing, out of the kitchen and up the stairs to my room, where I curled up on the carpet, sick with shame, wishing I could sink into the floor, into the earth, into the fire that was under that.

I cried until Jack gave up knocking, until the sounds of the dinner meal had come and gone, until Magic stopped whimpering for her late-night snack, until Dad finally came home and settled onto the couch in the den, and the neighbors' lights went out one by one.

I did speak to Jack again, but things weren't the same. We broke up after a few more months, and I was back to my presurgery state of boyfriendlessness. I tried to concentrate on getting my driver's license, working as a kids' party hostess, and figuring out what colleges I was going to apply to.

I'd been focused on Northwestern University in Chicago since I was in ninth grade and they'd sent me a pamphlet about how the school integrated the dramatic arts with a traditional liberal-arts education. Besides, Cindy Crawford and Julia Louis-Dreyfuss and the girl from *Father of the Bride* and a million *Saturday Night Live* people had all gone there recently!

I decided to try for early decision in the fall, but just in case, I would put in applications for a bunch of top-tier and midtier schools as well. Every school I was considering was at least three hundred miles away from home.

One morning, the school secretary paged me to come to the office between third and fourth periods. Lately, Mom had had this habit of calling me during the day. It was usually nothing. I had learned not to freak out the way I had the first few times it had happened. Today, I even stopped by my locker to put my math book away before meandering downstairs.

But in the office, which seemed unusually quiet for a morning in the middle of the semester, Sally, one of the principal's secretaries, looked wary. "Your mother," she said to me. "She sounds upset."

I picked up the phone slowly. "Mom?"

Mom was sobbing. "Ace? Oh my God, he did it. He actually did it."

"Did what, Mom?" I whispered, carefully stretching the phone cord so that I could move as far away from the secretaries as possible.

"Your father. He's leaving us again. I just got the papers."

"Papers? You mean he didn't say anything first?"

"Well, you know, he's been…he's been talking about this for a while." She sniffled loudly. "But I kept saying I didn't want a divorce. I may think he's a jerk, but he's my husband, and we said we were going to make it work. We have to make it work!"

I glanced around. There was a short, messy-haired kid, probably a freshman, sitting on the bench outside Principal Pauldine's office. He tugged at a loose thread on his Pearl Jam T-shirt, smirking and looking at me like he could hear my mother wailing through the receiver. I wanted to reach over and slap him. "Mom," I said hurriedly, knowing I was substantially late for fourth period. "Everyone gets divorced. It's no big deal. You and Dad are always fighting. It'll be better for all of us, don't you think?"

"How can you say that?" she shrieked. "It's the worst thing that could happen. I knew you would take his side. You probably knew about this already."

"No, I didn't; I swear," I said. "I'm just not all that surprised."

"I'm coming to pick you up."

I was left listening to dead air. "But I have rehearsal this afternoon," I said to myself. I handed the phone back to Sally. "I have to go home."

Sally looked at me sympathetically. "Is everything all right?"

Though things were rarely all right at home anymore, I had a standard response for any friend or family member or concerned adult who asked. "Yeah, it's nothing to worry about. We're just having a rough couple of months." No one wanted to know that the rough couple of months had actually been a rough several years.

"Okay, well, would you like me to let Mrs. Roche know?"

"That would be great, thanks."

I took the long way to my locker so I could avoid my friends coming out of French class. I grabbed my knee-length wool coat and, without putting it on, walked outside to the parking lot to wait for Mom. It took several minutes for me to notice the frigid air and my bare legs chattering together. Mom should have been there by the time I resorted to putting on my scarf and gloves, but she wasn't. I walked to the pay phone and tried calling home, but I only got the answering machine. Ten more minutes passed, and my mind started to race. I hurried back inside to the principal's office. "Did my Mom call again?" I asked Sally.

Sally looked up from her paperwork. "No, she didn't, sweetie."

Dammit, what if Mom had swallowed pills and gotten into the Subaru? What if she had swallowed pills and not even made it to the garage? Why didn't I have my freaking driver's license yet? How could I get home without letting anyone know? I didn't have any cash for a taxi, and it was too far, and way too cold, to walk. Another twenty minutes passed, and no Mom. I called Dad at work. I was about to start yelling at him for springing those divorce papers on Mom, but his first words stopped me.

"Ally, I'm glad it's you. I've had to put your mother in the hospital."

"Why?" I said, though I knew full well.

"She said she had turned the car motor on and was sitting in the garage," Dad said. "And without being there to watch her, I couldn't risk it."

"When?"

"She said she was going to do it right away."

"No, not when she was going to commit suicide. When did she call you?"

"About a half hour ago. I called the police and had them pick her up. She's in the ER at Suburban."

This was one of two times Dad and Mom's psychiatrist had her committed against her will. This was mainly because the criteria for involuntary commitment in the state of Maryland were among the strictest in the country. Hospitals routinely turned away obviously mentally ill people if they weren't convinced the individual was going to kill herself or someone else that day.

"This is all…" I said, my stomach churning. "She got the divorce papers, and I told her it was for the best. I never should have said that. And she could tell I was trying to get off the phone. She felt abandoned."

"Ally, the divorce *is* for the best, and if she really stops to think about it, your mother knows it too."

"I didn't listen to her, Dad." I choked on the tears in my throat and swiped at my runny nose with the faux-fur cuff of my coat. I was nearly knocked down by the mere idea of coming home and finding Mom dead in our garage, but at least she was safe now. They'd gotten to her in time, and it wasn't going to happen.

"Sweetie, your mom knows you love her."

"I have to see her."

"We'll go tonight. But right now I want you to go over to Andy's school and pick him up. I'll be there in a few hours, okay?"

I called the main number at my old junior high. The office paged Andy to the phone. I took a deep breath and told my brother about Mom, trying, and ultimately failing, to keep my voice steady. Andy burst into tears, and I had to hang up before I started crying again too. In the office, I found that Andy had told everyone that our mother had had a heart attack and was in a coma.

"I'm so very sorry," the principal's secretary said to me. "Please have your dad call us if there's anything we can do, and Andrew, take as much time off as you need, dear."

Andy nodded solemnly, and the two of us started home. "Why did you tell them that?" I asked.

"It sounds better than saying your mother tried to off herself."

I couldn't argue with that. "She didn't," was all I said.

Mom had apparently agreed to be transported to Sheppard Pratt Hospital, a mental-health facility in Baltimore County, after her initial evaluation in the ER. Late that night, Dad had a kid in each hand as we rode the elevator up to her room. But the second we saw Mom, we realized she had changed her tune and was already preparing to check herself out, her hair wild and her eyes bloodshot. "How could you, David?" she said.

"What did you expect me to do? We have children to think about."

She fumbled violently with a cosmetic case from her purse. "Funny, that never crossed your mind before. But the kids are growing up; they don't need me anymore."

"Yes, we do," I said automatically. Andy didn't expend the energy to say anything.

"If you weren't so scared of getting custody of them, you would have let me do it," Mom said. "But you're only thinking of yourself as usual. You betrayed me. I can't believe I ever thought we should stay together."

"The kids need a mother," Dad repeated.

I took Mom's hand, which she angrily shook off. "Mom, maybe you should stay for a few days," I said. "Talk to the doctors, get some new medication. It'll be a break, you know?"

Hands shaking, Mom dropped Visine into each eye. "Some break. This nut job down the hall tried to steal my clothes; did you know that? And the staff is downright rude. I got here, and they wouldn't let me out of the room, so I figured I'd sleep. Then an hour later, they tell me to get up so I can talk to some shrink. It's like they want you to get so pissed off you'll leave. Well, it worked." She wrinkled her nose. "Don't even try to tell me you don't notice the smell."

"Susan," Dad said. "Please. You need help."

"Not from you," she said shortly. "Get out of here, David. Come on, kids, we're going home.

"But, Mom," Andy said in a small voice. "You're not going to hurt yourself?"

"They wouldn't let me out if I was," she said. "And hey, Andy, I just thought I'd get a little brain tune-up here. But then I changed my mind!"

She chuckled at the pun and waited for Andy to do the same. My brother managed a half smile, but that was it.

Dad stared at her for a long moment, like he was looking for something. He knew that the exercise had been useless. Shoulders sagging, he said, "All right, I'll go." He looked at me. "If you need anything, you'll call me right away?"

I nodded, wishing to God that they wouldn't let us out of here.

Mom suddenly sat down in the dusty maroon recliner. "It means so much to me that you kids care. I've been thinking, you know, that no one ever really loved me until I had children. And it's really special." Her eyes moistened again, and she stood and scooped up her purse from the floor. "I bet I'll feel tons better after we spend the weekend together."

I mentally canceled my plans to work in the morning and go to a matinee with Tina at the mall. Following Mom and Andy out of the hospital, I wanted to bolt down a corridor and disappear. Even as the thought entered my mind, I felt horribly guilty.

In the car going home, I remembered the summer I was twelve. Mom had been visiting her aunt in Florida, and when she got back, I had left a pile of dirty dishes on the kitchen table. Milk was curdling in a half-eaten bowl of cereal, and insects were swarming around a pair of forks that were caked with dried peanut butter.

"Ally!" she'd roared. "This…is…so…disgusting!" Fueled by some insane anger, she'd grabbed the forks and chased me up the stairs. Breathing hard with terror, I'd managed to get to my room and slam the door shut. Unfortunately, I didn't lock the door, and Mom raced in and hurled the forks at my head. The tines of one had left a bloody scrape on my cheek that didn't heal for a week.

Why was I remembering this now? Did I want to hate my mother? Did a part of me wish she had killed herself today? What kind of awful person was I, anyway? I pushed the incident down even further in my mind and focused on the delicate snowflakes hitting the window a half dozen at a time.

It wasn't until we were home and Mom and Andy and I were in our rooms that I started to feel the anxiety, like I needed to creep into the shadows and listen at Mom's door every few minutes to make sure everything was all right.

Eventually, the chaos in my mind grew so deafening that I had to make it stop. I went into the bathroom and washed some old Vicodin pills down with a lukewarm cup of water. When I woke up thirteen hours later, I was horrified. I hadn't taken that many pain pills when my back was broken and I'd actually needed them. What was I thinking? My mother had a store of drugs for every imaginable physical and mental ailment, but there was no pill I could take for her.

My high-school career was coming to an end. I was going to Northwestern, and I'd missed being a valedictorian by one grade, a B I'd received for the gym class Tina and I had laughed our way through second semester sophomore year. I was a second-place salutatorian, but in a class of nearly four hundred, I was satisfied.

Mom's mother, the grandmother I barely knew, was dying of breast cancer. Mom, who hadn't been involved in her mother's life for years, suddenly didn't like the care she was receiving in New Jersey and moved her to the Village House assisted-living community near our house.

Overseeing her care was Mom's unofficial job, until she started dating a guy named Edwardo who worked at the facility. Even though now I had to listen to how much better Edwardo was than my father in bed, I liked the Hispanic guy in his midthirties. Whether or not he was right for Mom wasn't a major concern. The fact that he put up with her was enough for me.

That year, in high school at the same time, Andy and I grew closer than we'd ever been. I got him up for school as I had in the old days, and because we were in the same building, I could keep an eye on him. Since by senior year I was practically running the drama department, it was easy for Andy to join and get involved with the plays. It was the first extracurricular activity in his life that he'd stuck with. I wanted the rest of his high-school tenure to work out as well, but given that he wasn't the most self-disciplined kid in the world, and Mom didn't seem to care if he went to school or not, I wasn't hopeful. But I knew if I thought about it too much, I'd have second thoughts about leaving.

The last show of my high-school theater career was the musical *The Wiz.* I'd been up for the role of the witch, but the director had for some reason pictured me as the perfect Royal Gatekeeper. Tina was in the chorus, and the two of us had way too much fun going through our mothers' old '80s workout getups to put together costumes for the colorful show. On opening night, I sat in front of the mirror in my room, carefully applying moisturizer and foundation. I preferred to start my makeup at home rather than dealing with nonstop chaos backstage for an hour before the show started. I was humming along to Lisa Loeb's "Stay" when my mother did her typical thing of knocking and opening the door before I could say to come in.

"Are you almost ready?" she asked.

"Just about. Can I take the Camry?" I had officially had my own car for over a year, after Dad had bought me a used Toyota for my seventeenth birthday. But Mom was always finding some reason to ground me from it, so asking if I could take it had become second nature.

"Sure," Mom said, fingering her red plush bathrobe. "Is David coming tonight?"

"That's the plan. Him tonight, you and Edwardo tomorrow."

"I wish you'd asked me first. I would have liked to come to the opening."

I returned to my foundation. "I asked both of you at the same time. Tonight was better for Dad, and you said Edwardo had to work. Remember?"

"I could have come without Edwardo."

"You still can if you want. You don't have to sit with Dad."

"No," she said, sighing deeply. "Tomorrow's fine." She turned and walked slowly from the room. Her curly hair, which she'd started coloring red again after she'd met Edwardo, looked a little matted in the back.

"Hey, Mom? I meant to tell you that Mrs. August called. She wanted to know if you are coming to the Village House Board meeting tomorrow."

"Oh, that," my mother said flatly. "These people just don't get it, you know? I can't afford to waste my time on this stuff anymore. Your father's not supporting me. I have to get a job."

"When are you going to the temp agency?"

Mom narrowed her eyes. "I've already been there. But the technology's way ahead of me now. You have to know how to do more than just word processing. I'm lost, and I don't know if I can ever catch up."

I dusted my face with powder and threw a few bottles of hairstyling product into the tote on the floor. "You can take a course on that stuff," I said. "And Andy and I will help you."

"Andrew. Fat chance. And you're going to be gone in a few months."

She left the room and closed the door behind her. I spent a few more minutes screwing around in my room. Then I hustled downstairs and grabbed my keys from the counter. I'd just opened the door to the garage when I heard a horrible grinding sound. "Ally!" my mother said. "Ally!"

I closed the door and met Mom in the kitchen. "What?"

"You dropped an avocado pit in the garbage disposal!" She was nearly hysterical. "It's broken!"

"But I made that guacamole yesterday," I said. "I threw all of the pits in the trash."

"Well, you obviously forgot one!"

"Mom, it can't be that. Someone must have used the disposal since yesterday."

"No. Your brother doesn't eat, and neither do I."

"Well, it wasn't me. Did you see an avocado pit?"

"No. But something's down there, and it sure looks like a pit to me."

I admitted to myself that she was probably right. There was a decent chance I'd accidentally dropped a pit in the disposal when I was scraping the avocados. I did stuff like that without thinking sometimes. But I couldn't fess up to it now. I had to leave immediately, or I was going to miss my call. "Mom, that disposal's old. Maybe it just finally gave in. But I have to go now."

"That's crap!" she screamed. "It didn't give in. Someone broke it. You broke it! And here you are denying responsibility as usual."

I tried to turn toward the garage door, but I was rooted to the spot. "I'm not—"

"You are! And who's going to pay for this? You kids think money grows on trees, but we have a stack of bills, and there's no money. There's no money! We're broke!" Her voice had that familiar shrill quality that made me want to cover my ears like a little kid.

"I have to go."

"You're not going anywhere. You're selling that car!"

"I have to go."

She swiped at the counters wildly. Small stacks of junk mail and sticky notes fell to the floor. "You selfish—"

I knew it was now or never. I dashed to the garage door and locked myself in the front seat of the car before Mom could stop me. The car was sweltering in the early-summer heat, and I cranked up the air-conditioning until the beads of sweat on my forehead and the tears on my cheeks had nearly evaporated.

By the time I arrived at the theater, I felt dizzy, and my nerves had kicked into full gear. The cast had just started warm-ups when I rushed into the green room. Everyone was in costume except me, but I was mentally incapable of being embarrassed.

My mind racing, I tried to run through the routines I had in the show. When I couldn't remember a single one, I panicked. It was like those bad dreams that every stage performer has occasionally. Only this was real, and I was going on stage in front of five hundred people in fifteen minutes. In the women's dressing room, while sobbing uncontrollably, I vomited an unsavory mixture of half-digested yogurt and leftover guacamole.

"Ally, are you okay?" my friend Olivia asked when I emerged.

"I think so, thanks," I said softly, washing my mouth and hands in one of the basins.

Olivia smiled kindly. "I'm sorry. It's awful to get sick just before a show. Can I help you get dressed?"

Thanks to Olivia, I pulled myself together in time for my first act 1 appearance. And though I couldn't stop thinking about the fight with Mom and dragging my body around the stage took twice as much effort as usual, I managed to pull through it. By the time the last curtain fell and Dad presented me with a dozen roses, I felt like I'd been through a war. I had to get home.

"You okay, sweetie?" Dad said. "You look tired."

"Yeah, well, it's been a lot doing the show and working and wrapping things up with school and all."

"Well, the play was wonderful, and you were flawless as usual," Dad said.

My insides started to burn. "I better go. Thanks again for the roses."

Dad hugged me. "I'll see you and Andy this weekend."

I raced out to the parking lot without sharing champagne with the cast. At home, I found my mother sitting in the living room in the dark. "Mom?" I said, turning on the light.

"Turn it off. I don't want to talk."

But I had to. "Mom, I'm sorry. Maybe it was an avocado pit from my guac."

"You ran out on me. How could you?"

I sat down on the couch. My legs were cramped from the evening's dancing because I hadn't taken the time to stretch afterward. "I'm sorry," I repeated. "I wouldn't have, but I had to go. As it is I almost missed the show. I'll pay for the disposal, okay? We won't go broke."

Mom lifted her tearstained face to look at me. "Thank you. The show was good?"

"I think so," I said. I picked up on the change in my mother's tone right away and started to feel lighter, even a little hungry. "I didn't really notice. I missed you."

"Did David like it?"

"Yeah."

"I can't wait to see it tomorrow, really. What am I going to do when you're far away?" She started to cry again.

"Chicago's only a two-hour flight. You can come whenever you want." I laughed. "And hey, I thought you were dying to get rid of me."

Mom pulled me into a tight hug. My chest contracted from the pressure. "Oh, no, honey. Never. I don't know what I'm going to do without you. Do you really have to go?"

"Yeah, Dad already paid the first semester's tuition."

"You could still transfer. Go to Georgetown."

"Georgetown's not as good as Northwestern," I said. "Besides, by the time you get into the city, you might as well go to Chicago."

"Oh, Ally, please don't go. Please. I think Edwardo is getting sick of me. I think he wants to break up with me. You're all I have left."

"That's not true, Mom," I said, rocking her back and forth. But I had to admit that this wasn't a good time for me to be going seven hundred miles away. My parents' divorce was nearly final, and my grandmother couldn't have more than a few months left. My brother didn't want to have anything to do with Mom these days, and as the years went by, she maintained fewer and fewer of her friendships. If Edwardo left her, she really would be alone.

But I'd gotten into Northwestern, my dream school. It didn't matter that all the other smart kids were going places within driving distance—Penn, Georgetown, UVA, Duke. I'd been praying for the chance to get away for as long as I could remember. This was finally my chance to live my own life. I had to take it. Didn't I?

PART II

Still a little bit of your song in my ear
Still a little bit of your words I long to hear
You step a little closer to me
So close that I can't see what's going on
Stones taught me to fly
Love taught me to lie
Life taught me to die
So it's not hard to fall
When you float like a cannonball.

—Damien Rice, "Cannonball"

When I was a senior in high school, I used to lie awake at night and think about my first love, whom I somehow knew I would meet early in my college career. It was a major reason I'd decided to swallow my guilt over leaving Mom and go to Northwestern anyway. I'd had a few short relationships in the last couple of years, but even as I was dancing with a guy at homecoming or holding his hand across the front seat of his mother's car, I'd never been able to shake the sense of being wholly and completely alone. I was just months away from escaping the chaos that had been my home life for as long as I could remember, and I longed to be scooped up and rescued. I was run-down from so many years of taking care of other people and wanted someone to take care of me. I knew that things would change forever once I found that person, and I was determined that he would appear to me in the form of an eighteen-year-old boy.

In my daydreams, I concentrated hard to see what he looked like. But I didn't recognize him until the end of my first quarter at school, when I saw him in the Freshman Facebook, which in 1994 was an actual book.

I'd been playing around online in one of my school's chat rooms, which at the time were still a novelty. I started talking to this guy who could be identified only by his onscreen handle, "rjs242." He told me his name was Ryan and that he was a freshman journalism major. His jokes about his childhood in Long Island made me laugh, so I looked up his picture. He looked up mine too, and I guess he was pleased at what he saw, because within a few days, we were talking on the phone and then making plans to meet in person.

I walked up the stairs to Ryan's dorm at seven thirty on a frigid Saturday night in early November. I held my mouth shut to keep my teeth from chattering. There was only one crazy guy standing outside, and he was tall with black eyes so dark I almost couldn't see his pupils. "Are you Ally?" he said.

"Yeah," I said, feeling shy. "I guess you're Ryan."

We checked each other out. Ryan wore a long overcoat that he paired with a red scarf. "Well, so…" Ryan stuffed his hands in his pockets. I watched his breath travel out of his mouth and over my head. "Where do you want to go?"

I smiled and suggested Ambiance, one of about three decent coffeehouses in downtown Evanston. Ryan and I walked across town at a pace that was a little on the fast side. I noticed Ryan slowing down so I could keep up. On Clark Street, we met up with this guy from Ryan's dorm who wanted both of us to come watch *A Clockwork Orange* in his room after coffee. I was the first one to say we'd go.

We kept walking, the conversation gliding back and forth. We picked up right where we'd left off with our phone talks. I told him that my Ancient History professor claimed to have been cursed while on a dig near the Egyptian pyramids and that I was thinking of pretending to have Tourette's syndrome for a project for my Social Psychology class. Ryan told me that he didn't know what to do with himself now that soccer season was over. I told him about my friends Jasmine, Nora, Dorothy, Pete, and Leo. Ryan said that he didn't really like anyone on his hallway. The hot and smoky air inside Café Ambiance reached out and choked us as soon as we stepped in the door. I pretended not to notice.

"Do you smoke?" Ryan asked.

"Not really," I said.

"And you don't like coffee either, do you."

"Right again. But how'd you know?"

He grinned. "No idea."

Ambiance was structured like a fast-food joint. I looked at the long line of people waiting at the counter. I couldn't imagine where we were going to sit, as the place was already mobbed with big groups gathered around rickety wooden tables piled with day-old pastries and stinking ashtrays. I opened my wallet. "I'd better save the table," I said. "Can you get me a hot chocolate with whipped cream?"

Ryan shook his head. "I'll get it, okay?"

I nodded and watched Ryan's profile as he stood at the counter and tried to figure out what was drawing me closer to him. I started calculating how long we'd been out and started laughing.

"Something funny?" he asked.

"No." I stared over his head at the painting on the opposite wall, which looked old and expensive. A laminated index card right above it asked guests to please refrain from touching the art. I asked Ryan about his Mendocino Town Fair T-shirt.

"I never buy T-shirts," Ryan said. "But I really wanted to remember that trip."

"What did you do?" I asked.

"That was the thing," he said. "I didn't do anything. We stayed in this bed-and-breakfast in town, and I spent half the day just lying on the high bed in my room, listening to the music from the street. The people playing, they were pretty bad, you know? But they didn't care. They were having a good time."

I just looked at him without saying anything. I couldn't figure out why the occasional silences between us didn't bother the hell out of me. My eyes dropped to Ryan's hands. They were large and solid enough to be capable of hard labor, but it was clear from the smooth skin and neat fingernails that they never did any.

We emptied our mugs. I sat with both fists balled under my chin, listening to running commentaries on midnight rock painting and the latest Asian American Studies hunger strike delivered with Ryan's New York twang. Coming from someone else, that accent might have grated on my nerves. But when Ryan talked, it was comforting, like easy listening on the radio when you're driving alone at night.

The week before, Mom had come to visit me at school, because her boyfriend, Edwardo, had broken up with her, and she needed some "quality Ally time." The minute she'd unpacked at the hotel, she'd realized that she was out of one of her medications, and we'd spent the whole first day of our visit rushing around Evanston trying to get her prescription filled. The way she was sweating and crying, I thought something physically horrible might happen to her if she didn't get her hands on that drug. Even after she went home, I couldn't stop thinking about how I'd gone away to school and my mother had turned into a junkie. Until now.

Ryan and I must have spent a few hours at Ambiance, but I had no sense of the time. The longer we sat there, the more the background receded, and we seemed to be surrounded by empty space.

When winter quarter started, Ryan and I were a couple, sleeping in a twin bed together for several consecutive nights and going to each other's classes. I was having a grand time. It was a little like being permanently drunk. When I was with Ryan, I was euphoric, and the high went on for hours, regardless of what we were doing, and when we were apart, I counted the minutes until I could have that feeling back.

And then, one Sunday morning in mid-January, my phone rang at a few minutes after six. I rolled over and cuddled into the crook of Ryan's arm, breathing in last night's leftover Old Spice. My room-mate, Joan, was out of town visiting her boyfriend, so the machine was the only one that answered. The jerk kept hanging up and calling back until I had no choice but to pick up the phone. It was Mom.

"Hello?...Wha...what are you talking about?...Oh...I see...I wish you wouldn't do this...All right, I won't tell him...Okay, I promise... I'll see you tomorrow, then?...Yes, I promise...Bye."

The call lasted ten minutes. At first, Ryan was half asleep and not paying much attention to what was going on. But I guess he heard something in my voice, because by the time I hung up, he was staring me down over the pillow, and his fingers were encircling my wrist like a pair of handcuffs. I held the cordless in my hand for a second and then placed it carefully on the base.

"Al?" Ryan said.

"Yes?"

"What is it?"

The phone rang again. It was Dad this time, saying he'd found out about my mother's plan to fly to Chicago to say good-bye to me before killing herself in a hotel room.

"Dad?" I said. "Please help me. There's nothing I can do from out here."

"I don't want you to worry about this," my father said. "Your moth-er's just going off on another one of her dramas. How many times have we been through this?"

"No. I think she's really going to do it this time. She has very spe-cific plans, and you know what they say—"

"Honey, the only plan she has is to get you so worked up you can't think about anything except her. Let me take care of it."

I wanted to let Dad deal with it. But my father had a way of screw-ing up when it came to my mother, and I needed my last good-bye.

I caught a strand of hair sticking to the side of my face and chewed violently. "You can't," I said.

"This is ridiculous," he said irritably. "I didn't send you halfway across the country so you could be burdened with your mother's problems."

I almost laughed. Being burdened was the story of my life. "You can't stop her from coming out here," I said. "She'll think I told you, and then she'll hate me." I tried to ignore Ryan, who seemed frozen in position, his left leg intertwined with my right.

"What's going on?" he whispered.

"She won't hate you," Dad said. "The only thing I want you to do is call your brother. See how he's doing, okay?"

"Why don't you do it?" I said shakily. "You're the one who's there."

"I've tried," my father said. "He doesn't want to talk to me."

"Well, he's not talking to me either. Just don't say anything to Mom, all right?"

Dad said something about getting some sleep and concentrating on my schoolwork—got to show that calculus who's boss. Then I said something resembling good-bye and hung up the phone. I turned over, the panic buzzing behind my closed eyes.

"Are you going back to sleep?" Ryan asked me.

"Why not?"

Ryan pulled the pillow out from underneath my head.

"Hey!" I said.

"What just happened?"

There was nothing to say. Ryan and I were too new. He wasn't even comfortable with my need to brush my teeth before kissing him in the morning yet. "Never mind," I said. "It's early still. We can still get a few more hours."

"Ally..."

I looked at Ryan, my eyes pleading with his. "Please don't do this. Just let it go."

"Tell me what's happening with your family. I want to know."

"Trust me; you don't."

He reached over and squeezed my hand. "How about if you let me decide that?"

"It's my problem. I wish I could be you and not have to know any of it."

"Well, you're not."

"Right. Exactly. So if you don't want to go back to sleep, you can get dressed. Okay? I'll come over later, and we'll study or something. Maybe have dinner…"

"I'm not leaving." To prove this point, he got deeper underneath the covers of my bed and pulled me down with him.

"Ryan! Stop it! Don't touch me!"

Ryan gripped my wrist so hard it hurt. "Look, enough bullshit. Something serious is going on here. I know you don't want me to know about it, and I'm sorry that I'm here. But I wish you would stop worrying about what I'm going to think and let me help you."

I looked at him, and there was no question that I would tell him. I felt naked, like everything that was inside me was lying out in the open, right there for him to see. I almost had nothing to lose. Still, though, a huge part of me wanted to keep my mouth shut the way I had with everyone else my whole life. I fought with that part until I said, "Fine. My mother is coming out here to kill herself. She wants to say good-bye to me, and then she's going to swallow a bottle of pills at the Omni."

"Holy shit."

"I told you you didn't want to know."

"Jesus."

"I want to take a shower," I said.

"Wait," Ryan said. "Okay."

In the bathroom, I turned the faucet on scalding hot. I let my hair get wet but didn't shampoo it. I wrapped myself in a towel and slipped on my bathrobe, but I was still freezing. Back in my room, Ryan hadn't moved. I wrapped my arms around my shaking knees. "Won't you please go?" I whispered.

"Are you kidding?"

Then I was crying and couldn't stop. He just held me. "Ally, listen, no matter what happens, you know I'm here, right?"

"I shouldn't have left her."

He knew what I meant. "Yes, you should have. Because if you didn't, we wouldn't have met."

"This isn't what you had in mind; I guarantee that."

"It does scare me," Ryan said. "I didn't see it coming, especially at six in the morning. I'm not really sure what to do. But what I do know is that I would never leave you. It's all right to need someone, Ally, and I want you to need me."

They were the words I'd been waiting to hear all my life.

"Thank you," I said, half expecting him to vaporize right in front of me. After a few minutes ticked by, I couldn't think about anything except the warmth of his arms and the gentle movement of his long fingers on my scalp. I was hypnotized. I guess I fell asleep, and when I opened my eyes again, Ryan was holding my head against his chest so I could hear that he was still there.

We reentered the world around noon. Ryan fielded the phone calls and the questions from our friends who saw me looking like a ghost. Late in the afternoon, Ryan went back to his dorm to shave and get something to eat. I hoped he would stay there and do some work, but within an hour he was calling up from downstairs.

"I'm sorry," he said. "I just want to be with you."

For my family, it was another close call. Mom's psychiatrist had her committed again, and I knew things would be all right for a while. I saw Ryan every day the following week and tried to be really careful with him, worried that any minute he'd have a delayed reaction and freak out. But he just kept being there, and every day I loved him more for it.

January rolled into February. Ryan and I turned nineteen, and I started working in the psych lab of my Human Sexuality professor,

Dr. Murphy. Despite our crazy schedules, Ryan and I saw each other most days. Now that I'd gotten used to the high, I wanted to be with him all the time, and when I couldn't see him, I wanted to be on the phone with him.

My clinginess exasperated Ryan. But I couldn't help it. I felt like everything had finally fallen into place. Every day, walking to my morning class, I passed by Ryan's window and looked to see if the light was on. Sometimes I stood underneath the window for a few minutes and just gazed up. During my first quarter at school, I'd spoken to Mom every other day. Now, it took me several days to return her calls.

On a Saturday after breakfast with Nora, I stopped by Allison Hall and knocked on Ryan's door. There was no answer, but I heard Oasis's "Definitely Maybe" on the stereo. I slowly turned the knob. I was a little nervous about walking in there without permission, but I couldn't resist. Ryan had given me all sorts of excuses why we couldn't see each other that week, so it had been a while, and I thought if I didn't see him now, I wouldn't be able to get any work done that night.

Ryan was lying facedown on his comforter. We both loved that ratty thing. Ryan's grandmother had made it for him, and most of the colored squares were coming apart. I thought he was asleep, so I started scribbling a note on his desk pad. *Hi, honey, I was wandering around and thought I'd say hello, but you're sleeping, so call me later. Love...*

"What are you doing here, Ally?"

I looked down at my boots. "I don't know. I just wanted to see you, I guess."

"I didn't say to come in."

"Well, maybe next time I won't."

He turned over and smashed his face into the pillow. "What's your problem?"

"What's yours?"

"I asked you first."

I felt a sudden surge of panic. Someone, or something, had stolen my sweet and even-tempered boyfriend, and I wanted him back now. "My problem is that I try to do something nice, and you get all pissed," I said. "You could have locked the door or kept pretending to be asleep. Or I could just get out of here, and we wouldn't have to worry about it." I didn't want to leave, but I wasn't prepared to bluff. I edged toward the door, hoping Ryan would stop me. He almost didn't. I was in the hall before he finally came around.

"Well, you might as well stay a few minutes," he said.

"How gracious of you."

I plopped down in the reclining chair next to Ryan's bed and looked at him. "So how are you?"

"Fine," he said.

"I have a calc quiz tomorrow," I offered. "I'm freaking out. I mean, I can't believe I got an A on the last one, and the TA actually said, 'Nice job, Ally.' He knew my name and everything. Can you imagine if I pulled off an A in calc? My dad would shit a brick!"

"Yeah, that would be big."

I rummaged through Ryan's CDs and picked out the latest R.E.M. "Is this new?" I asked.

Ryan nodded. "A late birthday present."

"From who?"

"Nicole."

"Oh."

Ryan was staring at the Blues Brothers poster above his room-mate's bed. He looked like a wax figure in one of those museums.

"Where's Ben?" I asked.

"Out."

"Where?"

"No idea."

I couldn't stand it anymore. "Come on, Ryan!"

He looked at me innocently. "What?"

"Would you say something, for God's sake? Something's wrong."

He glared at me. "And what exactly do you want me to say? Being the expert you are, I'm sure you have an opinion on the matter."

I was furious. "Where is this coming from? And why are you in bed in the middle of the day? What's wrong with you?"

He swung his legs over the side of the bed. It was almost a violent gesture. "It's like you want me to be upset! Why can't you just accept what I tell you and leave it at that? Maybe I'm just tired! Christ!"

I tugged on the edge of one of my cuticles until it started to bleed. "You're a bad liar," I said softly. "If you don't want to talk about it, just say so."

"I don't want to talk about it."

"Fine." I stood up to leave.

"Oh, I get it. If I'm not letting you be my therapist, I'm not worth your time?"

I took a step closer to him and gently put one hand on his back. A wave of electricity, the bad kind, passed between us. I jerked my hand away. I sat down on the bed next to him and wrapped my arms loosely around his neck.

He didn't pull away this time. And so I waited.

"It just sucks," he finally said. "When you start thinking about something one day, and then you can't go back to where you were before you thought about it."

"What do you mean?" I said.

He didn't answer. I fingered the fabric on the underside of his rugby shirt. He leaned against me and let me hold him. I tried to figure out what could be bothering him, working it through like a puzzle. I fast-forwarded through what I remembered of our last conversation. I couldn't come up with anything out of the ordinary, but what if there was something I forgot? This had to have something to do with me.

I squeezed the cut on my finger so the blood gathered in a perfect sphere and sat back against the wall. The Oasis CD ended and geared up to repeat.

Ryan closed his eyes and opened them slowly. Then he whispered, "I love you."

"I love you too."

It was the first time we'd said this to each other, but there was nothing surprising in it. And it felt very right and very wrong at the same time. Though I'd been awake for a grand total of six hours that day, I felt like I could go to sleep right then. I sat up on the bed and reached for my boots.

Ryan gripped my arm. "Will you stay with me?"

"Don't you have work to do?"

"Why?" he asked. "Do you?"

I shrugged, and I guess that was all he needed. He leaned closer, and before I knew what was going on, he was kissing me like he was never going to see me again. I was just glad he wasn't mad at me anymore, so I kissed him back.

Things went back to normal for a while. Ben went home the next weekend, and Ryan invited me to sleep over. He told me to meet him outside the library at ten on Friday night. I put on my headphones and listened to some Red Hot Chili Peppers while I waited for him to show up.

I checked out my reflection in one of the windows. Under my enormous North Face jacket, I was wearing my favorite black jeans and a semi-low-cut velvet shirt. As a final touch, I'd spritzed on some Estee Lauder *Beautiful*. Ryan had a very keen sense of smell, and I hoped it would drive him crazy.

It had to drive him crazy.

The perfume evidently had the intended effect, because back in Ryan's room, he decided it was time we had sex. "We've been together for a while now," he reasoned.

"I don't know, Ryan."

As much as I hated myself for it, I knew I couldn't do it. I had no doubts about loving him, and I knew that he was the one I was supposed to be with, and yet something was holding me back.

We didn't feel much like fooling around after that. After we moved as far apart as was possible on a twin bed, a deep, unfamiliar sadness sloshed around in my belly. The night had been perfect, and I had ruined it. I lay there thinking about all the times I'd made fun of some girl for having sex with her boyfriend just so he'd keep coming by her locker every morning before classes.

The next morning, Ryan practically kicked me out of his room, and a nauseous feeling grew inside of me all day. Light snow began to fall around two o'clock. I kept leaving my desk to stare out the window. The lake was frozen over, and some little kids were trying to ice skate on the shallow part. What would happen if I went way out there and jumped up and down as hard as I could? Would the ice hold my weight, or would I be a goner?

I swallowed against the contents of my stomach and put my head down on the windowsill. I sat there until Joan came in. Then I figured I had to look like I was doing something, so I checked my e-mail.

The first and only message I saw was from Ryan. It said I was a tease for fooling around and then refusing to have sex. It said I was weak and dependent. It said other things about our relationship, some of them positive, but all I could see were the bad words, words that made me want to smash my hand through the window.

My hands shaking, I reached blindly for the phone, panicking that I wouldn't be able to get a flight home. And home is something that's always supposed to be there, like those packets of sugar on the table in a restaurant. It didn't matter that nobody wanted me in Maryland either. In the space of five minutes, it had become more important than anything that I get out of this room, this place, where all of a sudden there was this ugly person living with me.

I didn't tell anyone I was going except Joan, and that was just so no one would call the police. I got to my house at two in the morning with a temperature of 101 and stayed in bed the whole time.

Mom was cool about it. She was, after all, at her best when I was sick. Andy was MIA, and one could argue that my mother had nothing better to do, but for three days she transformed back into the mom she was when I was a little kid. She brought me hot tea with lemon and Theraflu and even called Tina and Kevin to come over and chat. They both told me that Ryan was an idiot if he didn't appreciate me for who I was. Kevin, who had decided last year that he wanted to be more than my friend, threatened to drive to Chicago and kick Ryan to the other side of Lake Michigan. Rationally, I appreciated the sentiment, but I was horrified at the thought of anything bad happening to Ryan caused directly or indirectly by me.

I went back to Northwestern, and Ryan eventually called me to smooth things over. Despite the instability of our relationship, we planned to spend spring break together at his house in Long Island. My calc final was scheduled for the day before I was flying to New York. I breezed through my other exams and spent eight hours straight in the dorm study room. When I finally dragged myself upstairs, I heard the phone ringing. "Hi, what's up?" Ryan said.

"Not much," I said. "Just getting ready for the big day."

"I know," he said. "I've been thinking about you all night."

I was warm all over and felt like flinging open the door and making sure everyone on my hall knew exactly how sweet he was. "Thanks," I said. "I can't believe you get to leave tomorrow. I'm so jealous."

"Don't be," Ryan said. "I'll just be cleaning."

"Don't go through too much trouble," I said. "It's only me."

"Yeah, but 'only you' has the highest standards of anyone I've ever met."

I smiled. "I like flannel sheets and my bagels toasted, and don't forget about the white noise."

"I'll give you a fan. Well, I just wanted to call and see how everything was going with studying and all..."

"Oh, wait," I said. "Could you bring over your vitamin C? I have a sore throat, and I don't want to be sick for the trip."

"Right now?"

"Sometime tonight?"

He hesitated. "I'm kind of busy, hon. I have to finish this European Thought and Culture paper, and I haven't even started packing."

"All right," I snapped. "Forget about it."

"Come on, it's vitamin C. Can't you get it from the dorm? You have friends."

"Yes, I do," I said. "But maybe tonight I want to see you."

"Of course. This isn't about vitamin C. You want me to come over. Why the hell didn't you just say so?"

"I really do need the—"

"Ally, I really can't come over. I'm sorry. I know you're freaking out about the exam, but you're just going to have to deal."

I couldn't resist fighting with him. "Last I checked, I wasn't begging you. I don't need you, you know." The statement was blatantly false, and yet I said it with total confidence.

"Look, I have to go," Ryan said. "I'll come by tomorrow before I leave, okay?"

In my room after the calc final had kicked my ass into oblivion, I had this sudden urge to sit down at my computer and write. Back around Thanksgiving, I'd had this idea for a novel about two college freshmen who find out they've loved each other through all these different lives. In each life, they have a major obstacle they have to overcome. But I hadn't gotten any further than an outline, until now. I typed until the phone rang.

"I'm here," Ryan said.

"Okay, I'll come get you."

Ryan gave me a big hug of congratulations. After we went back upstairs, he played Solitaire on my PC while I threw some clothes into a suitcase.

"Can I use the phone real quick?" he asked me.

"I guess." Why he would wait until he got to my dorm to make a phone call was beyond me. I returned to my packing. I wasn't paying attention to Ryan's conversation until he said something about being over at a friend's. Then I could feel my fists clenching so tight that my fingernails dug these little half-moons into my palms. I sat there fuming until Ryan finally hung up.

"What?" he said.

"I am not your friend," I said evenly. "I am your girlfriend. I have been your girlfriend for months."

Ryan clearly thought this was stupid. "Of course you are. Nicole said there's a They Might Be Giants concert at Loyola tonight. I wish I could hang around."

"Ryan, I can't believe you just said that. What exactly do you think is going on here? I thought it was a relationship, but maybe I'm delusional."

What was coming out of my mouth was loud and argumentative by anyone's definition, but so be it. "You know," I said. "Come to think of it, maybe you're right; maybe this isn't a relationship. Hey, I'm sure not happy. You've treated me like some kind of intruder in your life for the last few weeks. You don't even seem to like me, let alone love me!"

"I like you," he said, not raising his voice.

But there was no stopping me. "I've been trying to please you like some desperate female. But nothing's good enough for you."

"Al…"

"We can't go on like this. I can't take you calling me a tease because I don't feel ready to have sex with you. I can't take you telling people that we're just friends."

He stared at his feet. I couldn't believe it. It was like he didn't even care enough to fight with me.

"Aren't you going to say anything?" I said. "Fine. I guess it's the usual. I'm not privileged enough to know what's going on inside your goddamned head!"

"Ally, could you please stop?" he said quietly.

Stopping seemed like a good idea. Neither of us said anything for a while. After the initial dose of power I'd ingested wore off, I started worrying that I'd really blown it. I bit my lip and tried not to cry.

"Al?" he said.

"What?"

"I think…I think there is something I should tell you."

I watched Ryan's face wrestle with something I'd never seen before. I watched him until all of his emotions collapsed on themselves, and all I could see was fear.

"I think that if I tell you, it'll explain a lot. I wish I didn't have to, but you deserve to know."

Hearing him say that, I knew I wasn't crazy. There was a good guy in there; he'd just been taking a break for a while. But whatever made him come back was big, and suddenly I wasn't so sure I wanted to know about it. "What?" I said. "Do you have some kind of secret?"

I waited, but he still didn't say anything. We listened to the wind pressing against the window glass and the ticking of the heater gearing up for another round. Ryan wound his keychain around his index finger.

"Look," I said. "Whatever you have to tell me, it'll be okay."

For God's sake. I was softening already, and I didn't even know why.

The words came out in a gasp, like his throat was being squeezed. "I think I was born gay and raised not to be."

What?

"Oh, oh my God."

I burned a bunch of brain cells trying to think of something rational to say. I was a theater geek; I knew lots of gay people. In high school, there were the guys who were in all the plays with me. In those days no one admitted it, but we all knew. In the dorm, my friend Pete was one of the only straight guys on his floor. But Ryan wasn't like any of them. He was masculine. He played sports. He was hot.

How could this be happening? Why was it happening?

Stop.

I couldn't think about this now, because Ryan looked like he was about to be sick. "Well," I said. "You're still the same person. It's nothing to be ashamed of."

I refused to let it occur to me that I loved him—that the feelings I'd had for other guys couldn't even touch what I felt for Ryan now. He'd held this thing inside for God knows how long, and with a few words, it was out there, floating through the room like smoke.

"Does anyone else know?"

"No," he said. "I didn't want to believe it, you know? I wanted to be in love with you so much, Ally. Because it was, well, perfect. But I just couldn't make it work."

"It doesn't matter," I said. "I still love you, and everyone else will too. You'll see." I held him gently, and he buried his face in my chest. "Are you okay?"

"No," he mumbled. Our eyes met, and he looked regretful, like he'd just given up a huge chunk of himself. He saw that chunk floating farther and farther away, and with every passing second, it was harder to get back.

I wanted to feel better, because he had confirmed it. Everything that was going wrong between us wasn't my fault. Ryan didn't hate me for being an emotional basket case or not having sex. But my head was throbbing with pain I didn't understand, like he'd given some of what he was feeling to me. Both of us were crying, and we were holding on to each other so tightly.

I don't know how much time passed before Joan came back. She puttered around the room, hanging up her coat and checking messages like nothing had happened. Ryan tied his shoes and wrapped his scarf halfway around his puffy face and whispered that he had to go to the airport.

I walked him outside into the last of the winter. We were both soaked with freezing rain by the time Ryan said, "Al, I love you. I mean it. I know how it sounds, but what I said doesn't change anything. I love you more than I've ever loved anyone."

I stood there for a long time, my feet getting wet in the puddles, staring at his back until I couldn't see him anymore. Now that I was alone, I started thinking about how I'd talked to his mom and she had gushed that she couldn't wait to meet her baby's pretty, sweet Jewish girl from Maryland.

I felt my childhood instinct to fix what was broken rise up against my chest, and I considered running to catch up with Ryan. But I was nineteen years old now, and I knew that wouldn't do anything. So I sat down on the ground, wishing the rain would drown me. It had been less than a year since I'd started imagining my life at college, when love would make everything I'd gone through seem like a terrible but distant memory. I thought about how much I'd believed in that fantasy, and my mouth filled with bitterness.

When we got back to school for spring quarter, Ryan and I staged our breakup. It didn't surprise anyone given how much we'd been fighting. What did surprise people was that we were getting along better than ever now that we'd decided to be just friends. In our suite at the dorm, there was a rooming shake-up, and in a lottery Joan was able to score a single. Dorothy, who was not too fond of her alcoholic roommate, moved in with me.

My brother bragged to me over e-mail that he basically wasn't going to school anymore, because he couldn't get up in the morning and Mom wasn't making him. My anger at our mother for ruining his future led to a huge phone fight during which Mom threatened not to let me come home for the summer.

For weeks, months even, I'd been having this dream where Ryan was an old man. We were walking along Lake Michigan, and he was crying. He was asking me to wait for him, but I kept walking ahead. The first time I had the dream, Ryan and I were still going out, and he was lying in bed next to me when I woke up.

"What were you dreaming about?" he had asked me.

"You," I said. "What time is it?"

"Almost noon. Let's go eat. I'm starving."

"All right, let me just get a shower."

"Wait," he said. He'd pulled me close to him, and when we kissed, he passed me a red-and-white-striped mint from the cafeteria.

I started laughing. "Where did you get that?"

"Hey, Al?" he said. "Remember what you said yesterday?"

I didn't. He could have been talking about anything. "Sure."

"Well, I hope I wasn't being a jerk. It's just that, Jesus, you know me so well it scares me. I don't know how you get inside my head like that."

After we broke up and I started carrying Ryan's secret everywhere I went, I always woke up from the dream crying. That morning in May, my stomach actually hurt, like there were thorns twisting around inside and cutting everything they touched. I turned over in bed and saw Dorothy sitting in her desk chair. I closed my eyes again, willing her to disappear. I had joined the University Women's Choir last quarter, and that night I had a concert. I had to get dressed up in my long black skirt and white silk blouse. I didn't think I could do it.

"Are you okay?" Dorothy asked.

I pulled the covers over my head and tried to sink back into the darkness. "Yeah, fine."

"Shouldn't you be getting up? We're all going over to Pick Staiger in a few hours for your concert."

"No," I said.

Leo was hovering by the door. Then Dorothy was on the phone, and our friend Pete was upstairs in a light second. He sat on the bed next to me. "What's going on?" he said. "You've hardly gotten out of bed in days. We're all getting worried."

"Don't worry," I said tonelessly.

Pete looked mad. I thought he was going to lose his temper, which I had never seen happen. I almost wanted to push him. "Shut up. We're your friends. Remember us? We care about you."

"Thanks," I said, wishing I meant it.

"What can I do? Just tell me. I'll do anything."

"I don't know," I said. "Everything's fine. I just feel a little sick."

Pete glanced at Dorothy and Leo. He took a tissue and wiped some of the previous day's mascara off my face. "Come on," Pete said. "Let's get up."

"Nice try," I said. "But the answer is no."

Pete picked me up and carried me down the hall. I punched him with my arms and hurled mean words at his back, but it was like he didn't even notice. He turned one of the showers on full blast and dumped me in. I started crying, and I guess Pete felt sorry for me, so he threw me a towel and let me out.

No one made me go to the concert. I went because everyone would think something was really wrong if I didn't. But halfway through our program, I stopped paying attention completely and scouted out my friends in the audience. Jasmine and Ryan weren't even pretending to watch the concert. It looked like they were fighting.

Afterward, Ryan practically attacked me. "I need to talk to you."

"Now?" I said.

"You look terrible, you know that?" he hissed. "Your lipstick…it's all cracked like my grandmother's."

"Thanks, hon, you're a gem."

Nora and Dorothy and Leo tried to rescue me. "Ally?" Dorothy said. "We're going back to the dorm. Are you coming?"

From Ryan: "No. She's not."

"Come on," I said. "At least let me get changed."

He grabbed my arm. "Just when were you planning on telling me what was going on with you? I can't believe I had to hear it from Jasmine."

"I shouldn't have said anything to her."

"Well, at least someone enlightened me."

People were staring at us. "Keep your voice down," I said. "We're in public."

"I don't care," he said. "I hope the whole goddamned world finds out. Maybe then I wouldn't be the last to know."

I understood how Ryan felt. He'd trusted me with so much, and I couldn't even tell him I was having a really bad couple of weeks. "All right," I said softly. "Let's just go outside, okay?"

We walked until we stood on the rocks bordering Lake Michigan. The heavy wind whipped through my hair, and my choir skirt billowed around me like a collapsed parachute. Ryan stared at the Chicago skyline ten miles in the distance. "What are you looking for?" I asked.

He didn't answer me. It felt like winter on the lakeshore, so we walked to Ryan's dorm. We sat in his room, not saying anything.

"So…"

"I don't know what I want to say," he said.

"How are you feeling about things? I feel like it's been forever since we've talked."

"And whose fault is that?" he snapped.

"Ryan, this isn't about you," I said. "I've just been feeling like crap, and I didn't want you to worry. You've got enough to think about."

"You always think you know everything about me. It just so happens that things have changed. I've had kind of an epiphany."

I leaned forward in the armchair. "What are you talking about?"

"I'm going to start dating again."

"What?" I croaked.

"See, homosexuality, it's a phase for some people, something to think about and maybe try out. Like, last weekend, I went out with a guy."

"Wow. Really?"

"At first it was fun, you know? I thought I could be into it. But then he tried to kiss me, and I totally freaked." He shifted his long legs on the bed. "That's when I realized I must not be gay after all. It was a huge relief; believe me."

"Wait a second," I said. "Are you telling me you just decided not to be gay?"

"Well, that's not really—"

"You don't just decide these things, Ryan. Of course kissing a guy was weird the first time. Don't you remember the first time you kissed a girl? You have to give this a chance."

"No," he said.

This was conceivably the worst moment of the past week, and that was saying a lot. "I don't know how you can be this unsure of how you feel. What if you hurt another girl?"

He looked confused. "What do you mean, another girl?"

I realized that a part of me had never stopped being mad at him. "Yeah," I said. "You went out with me, and you were distant and mean, and that hurt me. Then we go through all this stuff together, and now you're telling me you're straight and going off to date other girls. How am I supposed to feel?"

"I don't mean to hurt you, Ally."

"That doesn't matter," I said. "You keep doing it, and I keep being accepting and supportive. But I can't handle you dating again, Ryan. It's not fair."

"Must you be jealous?" Ryan said. "We're supposed to be friends."

"That's not the point," I said. "You don't know what the hell you want, but you have no problem messing with other people's heads trying to figure it out. You don't care about anyone but yourself!"

Ryan's eyes widened. "What?"

"You never once thought about how being in a relationship that wasn't real would affect me. You just went along with it because it was a good cover-up for your precious secret."

"You think I don't care about you? You think our relationship wasn't real?"

I looked him in the eye. "If you were me, what would you think?"

We suffered through a few minutes of silence, and then Ryan just crumbled. He put his head in his hands and cried. I couldn't stand that those tears were because of me. "Ryan…" I said softly.

"Just leave me alone."

"I can't." I sat down on the bed next to him and put my hand on his head.

He shook me off. "Jesus, I can't believe you just said that."

My lips felt stitched together. I thought about a science project I did in ninth grade. It was about how astronauts lose their orientation to up and down when they're in space. That was kind of how I felt. I was lost in a black hole, and Ryan hadn't found me and dragged me out of it. He was going to date other girls even though the one who loved him more than anyone else ever could was sitting right there.

"It's how I feel," I said. "I'm sorry. I'm not myself."

"I know," he said, lifting his tearstained face to mine. "I've tried to be there for you. I get pissed when you don't let me. And you think I don't care."

He still wouldn't let me touch him, so I moved to my own space on the checkered quilt and let my hair hang down over my face. I begged Ryan with my mind to come over and almost collapsed with relief when I felt his hands on my back.

"Why are we doing this?"

"I don't know," I said. "But let's never do it again."

"Promise me you'll tell me what's going on."

"I promise," I said. "God, I'm so sorry, Ry."

"Me too, Al."

Mom had insisted it would be a good idea for the two of us to spend some time alone…in Tahiti. The minute we got on the plane at Reagan Airport, though, I knew she was in rare form. She needled me about the major depressive episode I was supposedly in and took me on a deluxe guilt tour of the horrors of her life since I'd left for school. After my grandmother had passed away, Mom, as her primary caretaker during the last five years of her battle with cancer, had been left the majority of her mother's money. Naturally, her brother and sister weren't keen on this arrangement, and they sued her. It had taken all of them the better part of a year to settle out of court. Financially, Mom came out way ahead.

Emotionally was a different story. She hadn't had a close relationship with her siblings for years, but now they wanted nothing whatsoever to do with her. She didn't have any girlfriends these days either, as there were very few people on earth who could withstand the constant barrage of phone calls, the routinely canceled plans, and the eventual blackening of their name that came with a relationship with my mother. Mom complained that everyone hated her, and my arguments to convince her otherwise were definitely on the weak side.

Nothing illustrated the decline in Mom's interpersonal skills better than the Tahiti trip. We'd been on the tour just one day, and all the other guests—most of whom were around my mother's age—began to avoid us, rolling their eyes when she would complain about a wait for a transfer or the taste of the water at the hotel.

It didn't help that my own patience for her had reached an all-time low. The night we arrived, I had a nightmare about Ryan and woke up clinging to the mosquito net above my bed, sick with jet lag. The dreams got so bad that I eventually stopped sleeping at night at all. When I got too exhausted to function, I passed out under an umbrella on the beach.

The last stop of our trip was Bora Bora, which did live up to its postcards. The palm trees swayed beside a lagoon of water so transparent that I could see the island's creatures playing among the coral recesses. I spent most of the days there wandering around the white sand beach, humming to myself. After two and a half weeks, I was in serious need of something to listen to besides my overplayed 10,000 Maniacs CD and my mother's whining. The night before our trip home, we were in our bungalow watching this tiny lizard climb up and down the walls.

"When's Ryan coming?" my mother asked.

"He's not," I said.

My mother yanked on a gray hair that had somehow escaped her colorist. "Didn't you tell me that you two were going to Ocean City?" Her eyes narrowed critically. "You haven't called him from here, have you? Ally, I am not paying for any calls that—"

"I haven't talked to him, Mom."

"But you made those plans months ago."

"I don't know," I said. "I just have this feeling that Ryan isn't going to end up visiting this summer."

"Did you have a fight?"

I sighed. "We always fight."

"You know, it really hurts me that you can't enjoy yourself," she said. "Do you know how many girls your age would die for a trip like this?"

"Yeah, well, they probably didn't have the kind of year I had."

"I knew it!" she said triumphantly. "You need antidepressants. But did anyone listen to me? Of course not. And now everyone's miserable."

"I told you I wasn't going to have a good time," I said. "But you wanted to go anyway."

"This is hardly my fault," she said. "You've always been mean, but I don't have to tolerate it anymore. Since you went away to school, I've changed."

I was glad my mother felt empowered even though, as usual, I had no idea what she was talking about. "That's great," I said. "I'm going for a walk, okay?"

I blasted more Natalie Merchant through my headphones and started down the beach. I watched the slashing waves at the breakwater and thought about our boat trip off the coast of Moorea when we fed the great white sharks. The guide had assured us that those particular sharks relied on tourists for their lunch and that they wouldn't screw it up by taking a bite out of one of us. But it wasn't like the sharks had told him that—how could he be sure? I had this terrible picture in my head of a shark chomping happily on one of my mother's arms while she howled.

When I arrived home after traveling for more than twenty-four hours, the first thing I did was check my e-mail. I saw the message from Ryan right away.

He'd done some thinking while I was away.

He thought I was manipulative and controlling, and that I'd sucked him into my dysfunctional world.

He didn't want to see me anymore.

He didn't even sign his name.

I sat there for a long time, my hands shaking, the words burning in my brain. Manipulative. Controlling. Dysfunctional. The rage boiled up and over. I typed the most vengeful letter I could come up with. He was a lying, uncaring, pathetic, coward. I regretted ever loving him. In fact, I hated him.

I sent the message.

I tried to shut down my PC, but everything was moving so slowly. I walked into the hall and stared at my mother's and brother's closed doors. I had only been there for a moment when all my senses returned like glass shattering.

I thought about how Ryan's e-mail could have been about Mom, and how Mom in turn would have written a similar response. I wanted to cry, but the tears wouldn't come. I was repeating the whole god-damned thing. At one time it had looked like I would survive, like I would come out okay, but the verdict was in.

In the bathroom, I sat on the toilet and fondled my pink Gillette razor. I wanted to die but knew I didn't have the guts to go through with it. I didn't even have that going for me.

Mom was not terribly sympathetic. If anything, she viewed the turn of events with Ryan as evidence that she'd been right about me all along. Mom and Andy banded together to make me feel like an intruder in the house where I had grown up. I'd never imagined the extent to which they resented me for going to Chicago.

The Saturday Ryan was to have visited me, I didn't leave my room. Andy came in around five in the evening with a cigarette hanging out of his mouth. He proclaimed me the most pathetic person on the planet. Then he left to score some more weed and smoke it in some dingy bar that he was too young to know existed.

"Ally!" my mother screamed from the kitchen. "Get your butt down here and put your bowl in the dishwasher!"

I didn't answer.

"I'm warning you," she said. "I won't tolerate having a rude slob living in my house. Don't forget for one minute that you are a guest here!"

I buried my filthy face in my hands, wishing there was some way to make myself disappear. The nausea that had been my constant companion for a week hurled against my chest again. I heaved into the wastebasket. Nothing came up. I hadn't put anything in my stomach in days.

"Ally! Do you hear me? Either you come down here and clean up right this second, or you're out of here! I'm sick of you lying in that room acting like you're the only one in this house. Get down here now or be prepared to face the consequences!"

When my dad saw me the second week in July, he pronounced that living with my mother was killing me. I'd come and live in his one-bedroom condo until I went back to school.

Dad didn't exactly have room for me, but he wasn't around much. He was working on a big project in his company's New York office and was up there at least half the week. The only issue was the sleeping arrangement. Before I arrived, no one even sat on my father's couch. After I tried to spend a few nights on it, Dad ordered a futon in the same bachelor-appropriate black-leather decor as the rest of the apartment.

Being alone all the time, I started feeling a little better. My novel about the soul mates was collecting cyberdust sitting on my laptop's hard drive, so I thought I would finish it. Once I got going, I worked on the book at all hours of the day and night. Kari and Michael were on their fifth life together and moved from college to graduate school to careers, all the while trying to reconcile their closeness with the fact that it was impossible for them to be together romantically. The more I worked, the more I wanted to work, and I was happiest when thoughts of my characters' lives replaced the concern for my own.

Dad decided I should visit my grandparents in northern California, and so one Thursday afternoon, I was packing while watching a Lifetime movie. The lead character had just killed her cheating husband when Dad's doorbell rang. I hoped whoever it was wouldn't make me miss the end of the movie. Besides, I didn't feel like talking to anyone.

Last night, I'd had one of the lucid Ryan dreams where we both realized we were there together, dreaming. And we could be happy, like all the pieces had magically come together, like all was right in our world, as long as we stayed in the dream.

I dragged myself off the floor. "Hello?" I said to the intercom.

"Hi," the voice said back. "This is Nick. I'm here with your futon?"

"Oh right, yeah," I said. "Come on up."

It took the poor guy ten minutes to appear from behind the queen-sized futon mattress. He was sweating a ton. We realized we knew each other at the same time.

"Ally!" he said. He pushed the mattress against the wall and looked me over, his hands halfway in the front pockets of his jeans. "I can't believe it. How long has it been?"

I laughed. "A good long while."

Nick Herrman was a good friend in junior high. We sat next to each other in most of our classes (Golden, Herrman) and went on a class trip to France together at the end of eighth grade. We lost touch when brilliant Nick went to the magnet high school in Silver Spring.

"What are you doing here?" he asked me.

"I live here," I said. "Well, temporarily."

"You used to have another house, right?"

"My mom still lives there. It's complicated."

He nodded. Nick wasn't a dorky kid anymore. He was at least a head taller than me, and his body was lean and muscular, no doubt the result of hours spent lugging around futons. He still had those impish brown eyes flecked with yellow and green.

"Well, I won't lie," he said. "This is a nice surprise." He turned his attention to the futon. "I guess I should assemble this thing, huh?"

I sat in the space where the futon was going to live. "You want something to drink?"

"No, thanks." He opened his toolbox and removed a hammer and a packet of screws. I helped him spread the wooden pieces all over the floor.

"So what do you do now besides put together furniture?" I asked.

"Not furniture. Futons. Only futons," he said. "Well, during the school year, I go to BU. I think I'll major in civil engineering; I don't know."

"You always kicked my ass in science."

"It's something to do," he said.

I noticed him staring at me, and I shrank back on the floor. "I guess so."

"Well, what about you? I heard you were at Northwestern."

"Who told you that?"

"Luke Kessler had a barbecue. I caught up on all the old gang."

"You're in touch with Luke?"

"Enough to get invited to his barbecue, I guess," he said, with a smirk that might have annoyed me if he wasn't so cute.

"Well, yeah, I go to Northwestern," I said. "I'll be a sophomore, which I guess you are too." I giggled self-consciously. Damn Ryan Stillman to hell. "I'm a psych major."

"Northwestern's a great school," he mused.

"Yeah, it's okay," I said.

"You seeing anyone there?"

I laughed to show I appreciated his directness, but it sounded bitter. "Not exactly."

"One of those, huh?"

"Yeah, talking about it kind of makes me ill." I wandered over to the kitchen.

"So ill you want to eat," Nick said. He followed me and rested his tanned arms on the counter.

"What? Oh," I said, remembering that there was nothing in the refrigerator. "You want some water?"

"You asked me that already," he said.

"I did?" I said. "What was the answer?"

"It was no," Nick said. "Well, let me just say, about your guy, it can't be that bad."

I poured some tap water into the only glass in the house. "You don't know that."

"Yeah, I do, actually. Last fall my girlfriend of two years and I started at BU together. At the end of the first week, I walked into her room and caught her hooking up with some guy she met at orientation. Now that's a good reason not to choose a college because of your high-school sweetheart."

"That's horrible," I said.

"I wasn't pleased," he said. "All right, it completely sucked. But I got over it."

"I guess that means you found someone else."

"As you would say, not exactly."

"Well, I guess I'll let you get back to work."

Nick nodded and sat down next to the futon pieces. I flipped off the screen saver and started chapter 9 of my novel. Within two minutes, Nick was looking over my shoulder. "What's that?" he asked.

"A book."

"You write books?" he said. "That's unique. What's it about?"

"It's a long story," I said.

"Looks that way. Does that really say two hundred eighteen pages?"

An hour later, Nick and I were sitting on the assembled futon. We could have talked much longer, but Nick had another job. As he was leaving, he asked me out. I said yes, rationalizing that I had nothing better to do. When I got back from San Francisco, we went to Dupont Circle and ate sushi. Everything was going great until we took the metro back and ended up at Dad's apartment alone, and Nick kissed me. We were about two seconds into it when I stood up suddenly. "I have to go to the bathroom."

I sat in there alone for ten minutes, chewing on a hair that had come loose from my ponytail. When I returned to the living room, Nick was stretched out on the futon with the TV on. "Come over here," he said.

I sat down next to him semireluctantly. I wasn't sure how I felt about this. On the one hand, it was pretty cool. After months of wasting away, this hot guy, who was interested in me for some unknown reason, had just dropped into my lap. But whenever I looked at Nick, I thought of Ryan, and I never wanted to love and hate another human being as much as I loved and hated Ryan Stillman.

Jay Leno finished with Jack Nicholson and went to a commercial break. "I still want that kiss, you know," Nick said.

"I want to kiss you too."

For the first time since I'd met him again, Nick looked unsure. "Are you sure?"

"Yeah, I guess so."

"Hey, I don't mean to pressure you. I just don't know why you're nervous. You're a beautiful and sexy girl." He undid my ponytail gently, and my long, brown hair collapsed down my back in waves.

The guy was smooth. Although we were the same age—I might have even been older by a few months—Nick seemed so much more confident and sophisticated. I looked at him doubtfully. "You really think that?"

"Sure," he said. "Even your old boyfriend would have to agree with me there."

I tried to turn away so he wouldn't see two tears that had escaped. It didn't work.

"What? What is it?" he said, anxious.

"Nothing," I said. "I guess I'm sensitive right now."

"About what?"

For a brief second, I thought of telling him. But then I remembered what had happened after Ryan had found out everything that was inside my head. All the things he knew could only hurt me now.

So instead, I smiled slowly and watched Nick's profile as he turned toward the TV, momentarily intrigued by Leno's next guest, a scantily clad Heather Graham. I kissed him on the cheek.

That was all it took. Nick came at me vigorously, and out of nowhere, sexual energy I never knew I had pushed me to want more, do more. It was like a drug, and it started filling up the gaping hollow space in my gut, kept on filling it, until I felt like I was overflowing. With Nick looking at me like that, responding like that, I didn't feel damaged at all. I felt perfect.

When I discovered sex, I felt like Indiana Jones with a secret anecdote to a nasty curse. The only thing Nick and I shied away from was, as they called it in junior high sex-ed class (which, ironically, we'd taken together), "intercourse." I couldn't lose my virginity, because I knew I didn't love Nick. Hell, I still thought about Ryan every day. A part of me felt guilty for doing this much with Nick, but it wasn't enough to stop me, because lots of hooking up made me forget.

The end of the summer brought two major developments. Nick went back to school in Boston, and Jasmine called to say that Ryan had shown up at her parents' apartment in Manhattan and insisted on talking about me for two hours. The fact that he could be sad, sorry, just like my dreams—it felt like I'd been buried under a huge pile of rocks, and someone had just taken them off.

Still, I was at school for a few weeks before I got up the guts to go see him. The day I decided to do it was Yom Kippur, the Jewish holiday of atonement, which I thought was appropriate. I went over to his new dorm before sundown, thinking I'd catch him before he left for services. I did not call up first.

He opened the door to his room, dressed in a dark suit that hung loose on his frame. I wondered how much weight he'd lost. "What do you want?" he said.

"Can I come in?"

He took a step backward and started to close the door. "No."

"Too bad," I said. There was no way I was just going to walk away. "I have some things I need to say."

"Well, I don't."

"You don't have to talk," I said. "Just hear me out, all right?"

He sighed deeply. "Fine, but make it quick; I have to go."

My heart pounded against my chest. This was definitely not going well so far. Ryan got busy cleaning his room with a vengeance, throwing stuff around like he was daring himself to break something.

I sat down gingerly on his bed. "I didn't realize you were still so mad."

"I'm not mad," he said. "I just don't see the point of you being here."

When I looked in his eyes, I saw nothing there. His face was a hard shell—maybe my Ryan was hiding somewhere inside and maybe not. "If you're not mad, why are you about to chuck those books out the window?"

"I have to go," he repeated. He glared at me, and I shrank back. I felt like I had killed his mother.

"Okay, I'll go, but can you just tell me what I did? I know we had a fight, but that was three months ago. I want to work things out, but I need to understand—"

"Look, if you don't know what you did by now, you'll never know."

"Huh?"

"And I don't want to work things out. I have new friends now."

I almost laughed, that statement was so ridiculous.

My reaction infuriated him. "As usual you have no idea what's really going on."

"I think I do," I said softly. "I've been thinking too." He sat down in his recliner, just staring at me. "Ryan, I'm so sorry for my part in everything. Not just the e-mail, but all the shit that happened in the spring too. The thing is, after you told me about, you know, I got depressed. Not just bad-mood depressed, but sick depressed."

I thought I knew what I was going to say to Ryan, but I don't know where those words came from. I had spent so much time trying not to be like my mother, and here of all places I'd finally I'd acknowledged the hideous truth.

"I'm doing something about it," I said. It sounded as if someone was strangling me. "I have an appointment with a psychiatrist out here."

"Good for you," Ryan said, like he didn't care one bit.

When Ryan and I were dating, I often gazed at his hands, holding them, touching them, admiring the elegant shape of his long fingers and the perfectly rounded edges of his nails. Now I imagined those hands reaching forward and scratching me, leaving five thin trails of blood on my face.

"I expected a lot of you," I whispered. "You couldn't cure me, and you couldn't be what I needed in a boyfriend. It wasn't your fault, but I took it out on you."

"That's the understatement of the century."

I hesitated. "But wait a second. We're both responsible for where we are right now. I tried to be there for you too."

"That's such bullshit. You never cared about me, and you don't now."

The worst part of it was, he wasn't just saying that because he was angry. He really believed it. All of those long summer nights had sure done a number on him. "Ryan, come on. Remember how things really were. Yeah, things were fucked up, and we did things we shouldn't have. But what we had was special."

I'd lost the nerve to say it in the present tense.

"Look, this is going nowhere. Will you please just leave?"

My heart was breaking. I stood up, barely holding on to the tears behind my eyelids. The holiest day of the year, the day of forgiveness, wasn't enough for me to get through to him. Either it was too late at this point, or it had always been too late. I wanted the last thing I said to him to sting, to get him back for being so damn cold, but my mind was empty.

That was the last time I spoke to Ryan, and my grief slowly hardened to bitterness, until I hated myself for ever letting him in, for trusting him with things that I had kept to myself for more than eighteen years, for thinking that he would save my life.

Nick and I flirted with what ended up being a bizarre long-distance relationship. I sat outside my room with the cordless phone, talking to him late into the night about Nietzsche, the Vietnam War, and Leonard Cohen. We sent snail-mail letters to each other once a week: "Dear Nick, today I was walking to Poetry class and passed a glass window. I looked at my reflection and decided that I was the perfect suburban college student. Leather jacket and boots, backpack slung over one shoulder, walking confidently, with a purpose, like I knew where I was going. And for the thousandth time I wondered what the hell I'm doing here." When I visited Nick in Boston, however, we realized that no amount of hooking up could mimic the attraction of the angst-filled letters. Things began to cool.

Once a week, I took the bus to Skokie to see a psychiatrist, who labeled me dysthymic (translation: having a chronic low-level mood) and rejection-sensitive (translation: thinking everyone was looking for an excuse to get out of my company) and drew pictures of my emotional life on a yellow memo pad. I told him that my friends, especially Jasmine, thought I was being distant and sulky, and he wrote me a prescription for the antidepressant Paxil. I'd been on it a few weeks when my high-school friend Kevin drove up to visit me from Maryland. We were at the movies watching *Get Shorty* when I started having trouble breathing.

Whenever I was around Kevin, I felt like he had all these expectations. He was still hinting that he'd do anything to get close to me in the romantic sense. And though I was more honest with Kevin than I was with most people—I really did consider him a good friend— the fact that he had all these illusions about me made me a nervous wreck. I didn't make Kevin leave the theater until I was covered in sweat from my forehead to my toes and was fairly sure I was having a heart attack. Back at the dorm, I called my psychiatrist, who announced that I'd had my first panic attack as if it was a rite of passage.

That panic attack was the first and last I'd ever have, and I'd never be sure if it was a result of the Paxil or Kevin or the general messed-up state of my psyche. But my mother, who'd started feeding my brother antidepressants when he was ten, was triumphant. I'd finally joined her club and was worthy of her love. We began talking on the phone more often, and she told me of her plans to begin substituting again and go out for Mexican food for her birthday. As usual, I was relieved when she seemed to be doing better, so I made plans to come home for both Thanksgiving and winter break.

Having learned that I would just stay with my dad if she got too out of control, Mom made an effort to ready the house for my arrival, setting out a green comforter untouched by cat hair and putting a note on the antique clock explaining how it worked. She'd started leaving little notes and quotes on stickies everywhere. The one taped to the dresser said: "It does not matter how slowly you go as long as you do not stop," Confucius.

Despite her efforts, as I walked around the house where I grew up, I noted that some appliances had broken, the furniture had a thick layer of dust, and every room was piled high with boxes of clothing and collectibles ordered from catalogues and QVC.

I remembered my mother on her hands and knees, scouring the bathtub once a week, and the gulf of sadness within me grew. She still wanted me to talk to her while she took baths in the tub, but now I made sure I cleaned it before any of us got in.

Around this time, my brother, more than a year out from graduation, stopped going to school for good. He and Mom lived in a state of total disarray, only occasionally leaving the house to grocery shop or make a pharmacy run.

One afternoon, as freezing rain threatened to stop up the gutters, Mom invited me into her bedroom. She was watching a taped episode of *All My Children* and asked me to go through a stack of made-for-cable movies and pick out one for us to watch.

I sifted through the tapes listlessly. "I don't feel like seeing any of these."

She patted the side of her enormous king-sized bed. "Come lie under the covers with me."

I did what I was told without saying anything. Mom's orange tabby, Tommy, nuzzled up to me, and I petted him absently.

She flipped off the remote. "You miss Ryan, don't you."

"Yes. No. I don't know."

"It's his loss."

"Sure."

"You are a terrific girl with so many special qualities, and now that you're taking care of your depression, I'm sure there are no shortage of boys who want to be with you."

We slipped so easily back into the pattern of something being wrong with me, and her rising to the occasion to fix it. I felt a pull to make things seem worse than they were, so that she would keep being my mom.

"I thought of a great idea for a book," she said. "I should write about my mother's experience with cancer, and how wonderful hospice was at the end. I could call it *Hospice, My Mother, and Me.* You could ghostwrite."

"You want to write about Grandma's death?"

"Her life and her death. Wouldn't that be interesting?"

"Maybe. It would be nice to do something together."

"Yes," she said. "I enjoy your company."

"Let's go to Walmart tomorrow," I said. The unpleasantness of running errands with Mom was only slightly outweighed by the relief I felt at being able to get her out of the house, at seeing her preoccupied doing the boring things other people did. While we were out, even for a short time, I knew that she would live.

"Your father isn't returning my phone calls anymore."

Dad had finally moved to New York permanently, and I knew that the last thing he wanted to do was get immersed in my mother's drama from four hundred miles away. "Well, he's busy with the new job, and besides, you guys are divorced," I said, as kindly as possible.

"The way he just left your brother was disgraceful. I don't know how he can live with himself."

Whenever she talked of Dad, it was with such loathing, and yet I knew that if he wanted to come back, she would probably let him. "He's been a bad father," I said, because this was what she wanted to hear.

Actually, though, I had mixed feelings about Dad's move. On the one hand, he had finally done something to change his life after complaining about it for twenty years, and it looked like he might achieve some semblance of happiness in the next decade. The divorce settlement heavily favored Mom because she was disabled, but it also meant that Dad could finally quit the job he'd taken solely for its mental health benefits. However, I also felt that by leaving Andy in Maryland with our mother, he was in effect sealing his fate.

Mom chewed on the side of her hand as she scrutinized the *TV Guide.* "My back is getting worse. I think those cortisone shots had the opposite effect. Between that and the prescription that made me break out in welts, I should get that Harris for malpractice."

"Mom, do you threaten to sue these doctors to their faces?"

"Sometimes it's the only thing that will get them to pay attention."

"Your back will be fine," I said. "But you need to do the exercises they gave you. The muscles are weak because you never use them. I remember some of them from when I had my surgery. Why don't we do them once a day until I go back?"

"I can do that." She smiled and moved soundlessly across the room to a stack of catalogs on the dresser. "Let's look at the new Victoria's Secret."

I eyed the glossy pages hungrily. Sometimes, if we'd just had a good conversation, Mom would let me pick something out. I pointed to a brown suede coat with faux-fur lining. "Do you like this?" I asked her, because if she didn't, I wouldn't have a chance. "This winter in Chicago is brutal so far."

I waited in anticipation as she considered it. The very idea of having a new and expensive item to wear around campus thrilled me. I understood a little how accumulating material belongings puffed my mother up and made her feel like a whole person, if only temporarily.

"It's very sophisticated," she said finally. "I'll order it for you and have it shipped to school. I saw these corduroy overalls that would look cute on you too. But first let me show you the fuchsia gown in the back. If I lose five pounds, it'll look fantastic."

Though the clothes Mom bought for me made up less than 10 percent of what she got for herself, she was being more generous than usual, and I wasn't about to rock the boat by asking her where she planned to wear another formal gown.

That winter, fighting against the feeling that I didn't really fit in at Northwestern, I decided to go through sorority rush. I finished with limited success but still managed to get a bid from Alpha Tau, where I was friends with several upperclassmen. I began the assimilation process I'd resisted during my independence-seeking freshman year.

My twentieth birthday was marked by a teddy bear from Nick that arrived in the mail, a group dinner at the Cheesecake Factory in downtown Chicago, and a new quarter of classes in my major of psychology. One course, Statistics for Psychology, immediately brought up bad memories from last year's run-in with calculus. It started off easy enough, though, and I took notes and checked out the guys in my TA section. There was one in particular who showed up late for the first three classes, wearing a seasonally inappropriate outfit of shorts and a T-shirt and dangling his rollerblades over one shoulder. He wasn't really my type—shorter and fairer than Ryan and Nick— but I thought he was adorable.

During the second week of classes, I was sitting on the stairs of my friend Jiao's dorm. Jiao had been dating my suitemate Leo for the better part of the year, and she also happened to live down the hall from Nora. Midway through our sophomore year, the group of college friends I'd have to the present day was solidifying. We passed around a bag of kettle corn and chatted about the formal dinner Leo's frat was having when up skated the guy from my psych stats class. Apparently, he was friends with Jiao. In my mind, it was the coincidence of the year.

Jiao introduced us, and I said hi. My cheeks were pink, and I couldn't even look at him. We all talked for a few minutes. His name was Jesse, and he was, typically, from California. He was a psychology major too, and we had another class together that quarter. I felt immediately drawn to him, my world suddenly a kaleidoscope of color. But since Jesse had a girlfriend and I was still sort of with Nick, I felt sure that nothing could come of it.

Jiao and Leo did not agree, and they planted enough seeds so that the possibilities started to take root in our minds. Dad had given me a pair of rollerblades for my birthday, and we spent those first prematurely warm and sun-drenched March afternoons cruising around campus, holding hands in an I'm-just-trying-to-keep-upright-this-doesn't-mean-anything way.

It was two in the morning, and Jesse and I had known each other a little more than a week. Our first Abnormal Psych test was the next morning, and we were sitting on one of the uncomfortable sectional couches in the study lounge in my dorm's basement, our shoeless feet propped up on the coffee table. I had been combing the first third of the text for the last couple of days, memorizing hundreds of bolded terms and their definitions.

Jesse glanced at the pages written in my tight script. "Dude, don't you think you're overdoing this a little?" he said.

"Yeah, well, unlike some people, I can't just show up at lectures and absorb everything."

"Neither can I," he said.

"Whatever. I know the truth about you."

"Right. I went to Catholic school for twelve years. I was a nerd. This is college. I want something else."

I nodded. "Well, I wish things came more easily to me. The only reason I got into this school is that I studied twice as hard as everyone else."

"You sure are hard on yourself."

I stared at him for a moment and then said, "Hey, want to see something cool?"

I produced an art poster of eight pairs of eyes from a stack in the corner. Jesse looked it over. "Someone in your dorm did this?"

"Yeah. Look closer."

He pointed to the last pair in the third section. "Is that you?"

"Uh huh. He said he took a few hundred photos, and I made the final cut."

"They're pretty," he said. "Green and kind of…gold." He said it factually but moved a little closer to me on the couch. "I should probably go home, but I don't want to."

"Are you ready for this thing?"

An easygoing laugh: "Not really."

"Why are you a psych major anyway?"

"Good question. I don't know. I took a class. It was interesting. I won't have to spend every day plugging shit into formulas."

I thought of my own reasons for becoming a psychology major, and then I was so tired I could barely hold up the ten-pound textbook. I rubbed my eyes and read a passage on phobias aloud to Jesse. "Individuals with social phobias have an extreme fear of social situations and of embarrassing themselves. The most common types of this phobia are public speaking and eating in public."

"Eating in public? Like in the high-school cafeteria?"

"I always hated that, even when my friends had the same lunch period. I used to come up with excuses not to go. I wonder why."

"I don't know. Are you a social misfit?"

I grinned. "Possibly. What do you think?"

"I think…not." He reached over and kissed me, soft and tentative. I closed my eyes and slid my arms around his neck. "I'm sorry," he said, after a minute.

"Why? I wanted to."

"Me too. Obviously."

After that night, life began to accelerate, one day crashing into another. Our chemistry, which we gave in to repeatedly during long nights in Jesse's room at his fraternity house to the soundtracks of Sarah McLachlan and Tori Amos, was the foundation on which everything else was built. For the first time in my life, I realized what it was like to have no control over my impulses or actions, and not to want any. Jesse's breakup with his girlfriend and my casual e-mail to Nick barely registered.

Jesse seemed to view the world simply, his life a series of daily events that progressed in no particular order. He made friends easily—testing the mood of any place he entered and then leaving behind him a soil from which new relationships would spring.

When he looked at me, his face awash with quiet desire, I felt myself being made over into the girl I'd always wanted to be: a girl who took off on a spontaneous road trip to Indianapolis, who left a boring lit class early to walk through the riot of color in the Shakespeare gardens with my headphones blaring, who laughed uproariously at the letters to the editor published in the campus daily, and who bought a dress for a sorority formal the same morning.

March gave way to April and then May, and Jesse and I wasted time pushing each other on the swings in one of the Evanston parks, listening to the wind playing in the treetops and drinking vodka from a flask.

We went to Jesse's fraternity formal and then Alpha Tau's. At these events, we often snuck out to be alone. My Alpha Tau pledge mom took a photo of us dancing close on the ballroom's balcony, which she later hung in our house's parlor with the caption: "Young love." I wasn't even mortified.

One afternoon, we were lying on top of the flat comforter on Jesse's twin bed. I watched him drop off to sleep with his arm flung across my lap. It twitched slightly as he completely relaxed. Outside, the sun was still in the moment just before it dipped behind the clouds. The natural light in the room was fading when, lashes fluttering, Jesse told me he loved me. I smoothed down the damp, sandy hair on his forehead and whispered it back.

In the evenings we'd get up and drive off on an adventure with Jesse's friend Raj and his girlfriend. On our way to Wisconsin to buy cheese, or into an obscure Chicago neighborhood to bowl, Jesse and I would curl up in the backseat with the windows all the way down, the drums of U2's "Hawkmoon" thundering in the speakers. Resting my head on his shoulder and feeling the light warmth of his skin against mine, I found that I could breathe—taking in one huge, satisfying gulp of air after another.

Jesse drove me in his little blue Ford Escort to see my psychiatrist once a week, waiting for me in the parking lot or running errands until I was done. On the way back to campus, he never asked questions, for which I was grateful. Though I was openly expressive in my love for him, writing him rather eloquent notes about how he'd changed my life, it was still my mission to cover up everything inside me that was broken and had the potential to drive him away. After one appointment, Jesse made a detour and drove along Lake Michigan, stopping on the side of Sheridan Road and turning off the ignition.

We were listening to Peter Gabriel's "Don't Give Up," and Jesse was looking straight out the windshield, pensive, borderline sad.

"What is it? What's wrong?" I said.

"I really like this song."

"Me too."

His cool green eyes met mine, and I wanted to ask him why this song of insecurity and desperation, two qualities I in no way associated with Jesse, resonated, but I couldn't find the words. So I just held his free hand and passed him a half-empty can of Mountain Dew. And everything was as before.

A few weeks from the end of the school year, I found out I hadn't been accepted into Northwestern's fiction-writing program. It wasn't a surprise. Not only was it extremely competitive, but I'd also put on the application that I would do a double major with psychology, which was frowned upon. Nevertheless, academic failure was something I'd never experienced, and I called my mother, devastated.

"But I finished a novel," I said, the tears in full force. "And they still didn't accept me. They must think it's awful."

"Your fiction is very good, Ace," Mom said. "Your teachers have always said so."

"Yeah, but this is college, and they know what they're talking about."

"You will always be a writer, but not being in this program means you'll be well rounded. This is God's way of telling you that you need to have other things in your life. And you do."

I sniffled. "Like what?"

"Well, take Jesse for instance. Would you trade your relationship with him for a spot in this writing program?"

"No," I said. "I love him."

Mom had started taking a new drug, Stadol, allegedly for the pain in her back. Half the time, when I talked to her, she sounded high or was on a crying jag because she'd skipped a dose. But she still knew exactly the thing to say in situations like this. She knew that to be in a romantic relationship that was working was something I'd wanted for a long time, and that with Jesse I was happier than I'd ever been. She knew that yet another academic achievement didn't remotely compare, and she'd reminded me of that. When I hung up the phone, I wasn't upset about the program anymore, and I thanked God for Jesse and the fact that my mother could still be there for me.

In June, I went home to do an internship at the Association for Interactive Media in DC. In 1996, the Internet wasn't a mainstream thing, but I'd been interested in it since its early-'90s incarnations as bulletin-board systems where people would get together and chat through their computers. The association was researching what the Internet would do for society in the future, and I was captivated, often staying in our office on P Street late at night to analyze trends from years of news articles and input my findings into a massive Excel database. Jesse stayed in Evanston to work as a counselor at Northwestern's overnight camp for gifted elementary-school kids.

The second week after I'd left him, I came home from work and found him hiding under my bedcovers with a bouquet of roses. He'd driven the twelve hours from suburban Chicago to suburban

Maryland in one day, just because he'd missed me. Learning that Mom and Jesse had worked together to bring him here, my expression was pure joy, captured in several photos from my mother's camera. I wasn't even worried about what she might have told him when I wasn't around.

In those moments, I decided that we would have sex that weekend. My virginity no longer seemed like something I needed to protect. I was in love, and it was time. After a day of wandering around DC and showing Jesse off to Tina and Kevin, we lay together quietly in my bed. As we moved together, I thought my tears were from the pain, which, though intense, probably wasn't any different from what everyone else felt the first time. I didn't understand that my emotion was coming from another place entirely, from the part of me that was terrified of where the depth of my feelings for him was going to lead.

Jesse's presence sustained me for a while after he went back to Chicago. I sang in the shower, invited my friends to the Kings Dominion amusement park to ride the upside-down roller coasters, and spent my Metro Red Line commutes dreaming of what we'd do the next time we saw each other. Neither my mother nor my brother really appreciated seeing me happy for so long, though, and hostilities ensued.

"Your brother doesn't like you," Mom proclaimed one day.

"Well, I don't know why. I've always been perfectly nice to him." My tone was defensive, because I recognized a kernel of truth. When I'd knock on Andy's door to play Nintendo or just hang out, he'd often pretend he didn't hear me, and he would rather die than have me around when his friends were over.

"He says you're just using us for a place to live this summer."

"Some people are still in school. And this is my home, I thought."

She treated me to her best beleaguered look. "Andrew's going to finish the basement and start a business down there," she said. "Why can't you do something useful like that instead of that Internet thing that doesn't pay?"

"It pays in experience." I was getting really aggravated, so I turned my attention to the Gap box on my bed. I'd seen a really cute tank top while I was shopping with Tina, and I'd bought it for Nora for her birthday. "Do you have any wrapping paper?"

Mom pounced on this. "Tell me that's not another gift for one of your friends. I find it funny that you're always asking to borrow from me, and yet you have no qualms about spending money on everyone under the sun."

"It only cost ten dollars," I said, as if that would be a valid argument in her mind.

"You need to get your priorities straight."

I sighed. "Okay, Mom."

Toward the end of July, things with Jesse's kids got very hectic, and he was only able to talk to me a few times a week. When I did manage to pin him down, our conversations were suddenly stilted and distant. I didn't realize how much of our relationship was based on the ease of proximity until we had to sustain it over hundreds of miles. I tried to make myself believe that I was imagining Jesse's flagging interest, but my anxiety only increased.

When I told Jasmine about it, she said that I should talk to Jesse. She thought I should tell him outright that I needed to be reassured. I fought against this for a few weeks, until it occurred to me that I might lose Jesse in the process of protecting him from the real me.

"It feels like you're avoiding me," I finally said one night in early August after it took him three days to return a call.

He said nothing.

I took a deep breath. "Maybe it's wrong to be insecure. But I guess that sometimes, I just feel that you're not even thinking about me. It would make me really happy if you could call me a little more."

"I'll try," he said, but his voice was noncommittal.

We had several more conversations like this, all initiated by me. In each one, Jesse sounded farther and farther away, and in each one, a little more bitterness crept into my voice.

Where had I gone wrong? Was it in allowing myself to get close to him in the first place? Was it in revealing even a tiny part of the emotion that had been locked in my heart since Ryan had turned on me? Or was it just something sour Jesse could sniff out in my genes?

Despite Jesse's hints that I should stay where I was, I flew to Chicago to visit him. His camp was on hiatus for the weekend, and so the two of us were alone in the dorm. Jesse's lack of response when I touched him felt like I'd been punched in the stomach. The distance between us opened up and deepened.

We sat under the afghan on his bed, listening to The Cure's "Wish." I'd just taken a shower, and the sound of dripping water echoed off the tiles. I stared at the wall in front of us and imagined the clean white paint littered with cracks.

"Why are you being like this?" I asked.

"I don't know."

I wanted so much to fight against the onset of drama, but the anger was rising in me like a wave. "Have I really asked for so much?"

"No."

"What do you want me to do, Jesse? You want to know why I'm mad? I'm mad because my whole life has been a fucking disaster."

"Your life isn't a disaster. Why do you say stuff like that?"

I realized that from his perspective, it was probably true. When I talked, it was about us, and there it stopped. I swatted at fresh rounds of tears slipping down my cheeks, hating that I was, once again, in a situation that reeked of how my mother managed to destroy perfectly good relationships without even trying. "Never mind. Just tell me how this got so screwed up."

"It's not your fault. It's mine."

"Tell me why."

I looked at him, at the pain standing naked in his eyes, and his face was Ryan's, and I was back in the moment over a year ago, when I'd been powerless to stop my heart from breaking the first time. My mother's voice, the one she used to hurt me, sounded in my ears. "Do it to me once, shame on you. Do it to me twice…"

"I just…I know you're pissed at me, and I can't stand it, so I want to get away. That's just the way I am."

Somehow, he knew how much I needed to hear that I wasn't some kind of toxin, and so he'd taken a step onto the ledge. But that might have been the most he'd disclosed to anyone, and he couldn't go further. So we stalled there.

Jesse's older friend Brad drove me to the airport the next day. "He loves you, but your relationship is changing, and he doesn't know how to deal with that."

"He won't learn, Brad."

He sighed. "I know."

Back home, I started going out a lot. My fellow interns at the association were well connected at Georgetown and the University of Maryland, and there were parties on fraternity row every night of the week. I had this irresistible pull to feel attractive to the opposite sex, and because of that, combined with the fact that I needed to escape myself at any cost, I drank too much and ended up dancing, barely standing, in the arms of some guy I didn't know. One night I had so much tequila that I had to call my brother from a stranger's car phone and beg him to pick me up.

I didn't talk to Jesse for two weeks, but we stayed together after returning to school. It reminded me of the last few years of my parents' marriage—my father totally checked out, my mother reluctant to cut the cord lest she spontaneously discover some magical way to get him back. When I'd visit Jesse in his new apartment off campus, I'd try to be on my best behavior even as he continued to not care, and my fury at his not caring simmered. I'd moved into the sorority house, and I kept busy with that as well as my new classes.

In November, at a party Jiao had at her apartment, after another fight that left both Jesse and me exhausted and numb, we decided that we were done. I used the opportunity to get drunker than I'd ever been and was in such bad shape I almost didn't make it home. An hour later, Jesse and his friend Raj rang the doorbell of the sorority house. I stumbled downstairs, eyes bloodshot and breath bitter.

"Are you okay?" Jesse asked softly.

"No," I said. "But you're not going to do anything about that, are you?"

And he didn't. But Raj came back the next day without Jesse, and without making the effort to see through my own pain, I hooked up with him. It happened a few more times, and when it was over, my self-loathing returned to post-Ryan levels.

Jesus Christ. When had I become the type of person who made out with her boyfriend's best friend? I saw the situation for what it was. My love hadn't reached Jesse, my suffering hadn't changed him or even wounded him really, so I would betray him to get the reaction I wanted.

I had a single room in the house that quarter, and as the days turned colder, I spent a few minutes every night kneeling beside my bed, my hands clasped together like an observant Christian kid. I'd started thinking of Ryan again nonstop and had written him a few letters that I couldn't get the nerve to send. No matter how many times I told myself that he didn't deserve this real estate in my mind, I couldn't seem to shake him from my soul.

I called Mom. "I think coming back here might have been a mistake."

"I knew it was. Every summer you talk about transferring, and every fall you go back."

"I just...I really thought joining a sorority would give me some-place to belong, but a lot of the girls I really liked graduated last year. Some of the people who live here want to go out and party every night, and some of them are so conservative they get all offended if you kiss in front of them. I can't relate to anyone. I'm lonely. I hate it."

"Girls are fickle, and you've had problems with friendships since you were little," she said. "And I'm sure seeing Ryan—and now Jesse—every day doesn't help matters."

"I don't see them that much, but you wouldn't know it given how much I think about them. I keep trying to figure out what I did to deserve all this."

"You depended on them too much," Mom said. "And they were too immature to handle it, so they left."

"Dr. Cooper says I keep picking these emotionally unavailable guys."

"Well, that's no surprise. You're looking for a man like your father. At least you've only stayed with these boys for a few months. I wasted twenty-five years of my life being abused."

When a relationship went bad in my mother's life, she just blamed the other person. But I knew better. I knew that the problem was me, that I was poison.

If only I wasn't so emotional, if only I didn't care so much, if only I could change so that guys would want to love me instead of having casual fun for a little while and then leaving because they couldn't stand knowing me. I'd never been much of a believer, but I was desperate enough to appeal to a higher power to release me from the agony that had become synonymous with relationships. I whispered the prayers every night.

The middle of my junior year brought my election to the executive board of the Panhellenic Council, the body that governed all the sororities on campus. January was my first sorority rush on the "other side," a weeklong process of constant parties during which we were expected to entertain four hundred eighteen- and nineteen-year-olds and convince at least thirty of them to start spending all their free time at our house.

The parties were all the same. We'd lean over the railing at the top of the staircase and look out at the sea of pretty heads. The clashing scents of perfumes and shampoos always threatened my nose, and I would stand there twitching until the sneeze passed. The chatter was an appropriately fixed volume—loud enough so the girls freezing outside could hear what a jovial place Alpha Tau was to be, yet soft enough so my sisters and I could absorb the rain of instructions.

All of us were dressed in regulation clean, well-fitting blue jeans and skirts and not-too-form-fitting blouses. We wore the right amount of makeup and jewelry and smile. In the living room, the scent of brewing coffee and wood burning on the fireplace created the desired homey atmosphere.

Conversations with the visiting girls took place in a fixed, orderly manner, and I'd proceed to my meetings while squinting at a little slip of paper that told me to meet rushee number five in the formal room with the piano. The girl and I would sit gingerly on the floor, spread our long skirts around us as if posing for a picture, and proceed to talk about her major, her hometown, and whether she preferred skiing at Stowe or Vail.

It felt like an eternity before Bid Day was upon us and we welcomed our thirty new members with ecstatic hugs and lettered sweatshirts. Those gifts, however, were nothing compared to the promise of men. At the end of the night, ten fraternities would arrive on our doorstep and to sing to the girls, and so the new pledges impatiently endured constant pictures and storytelling sessions waiting for the guys to show up.

I achieved my goal for the serenade, which was to avoid running into Ryan, and was in fairly good spirits when our party partner for the night, the Delta Omega fraternity, finished singing and fifty-plus guys crowded into our basement with paper cups of hot chocolate. The scene was total chaos, and despite the fact that all anyone wanted to do was go back to the Delta Omega house and get hammered, the group just couldn't get its act together to leave.

So this one guy stood on a chair and ordered everyone out. And everyone just magically followed him like he was the Pied Piper. I dispassionately observed that he was good-looking, more Jesse than

Ryan with a shorter, muscular build and intense blue-gray eyes. I walked up and asked him how he happened to command that much authority, even among the girls. He said modestly that he was a fifth-year senior, and so he'd been around a while.

He told me his name was Sam, and walking up to the fraternity, and then inside the fraternity, it was like there was no one else there. The guy wanted to know everything about me, asking about my classes, my friends, and my childhood. For reasons I couldn't understand, answering his questions semihonestly, although with a slightly sarcastic bent, seemed easy and natural. We were both Russian Jews from the East Coast and therefore shared many of the same cultural associations, and the more I listened to him and got a sense of what made him tick, the greater the sensation that I had just met the male version of myself.

All the guys I'd dated in college were wicked smart, but Sam was driven and proud of it. He'd stayed at school an extra year to do a double major in music history and bioengineering and was writing a senior thesis for each one. He was resolute that he wanted to go to graduate school, become a professor, and play saxophone on the side. I learned that he'd had what he considered terrible luck with women through his college career, and his current attitude toward my sex was bitter and borderline contemptuous. My recent relationship failures still fresh in my mind, this admission drew me closer to him, as did our mutual curiosity about the tall, blond, nonneurotic Midwesterners that greatly outnumbered people like us on the Northwestern campus.

We'd arrived at Delta Omega around eleven, and the next time I looked at my watch, it was close to four. My sisters had left for the sorority quad in dribbles over the last few hours, smiling at Sam and me sitting on the couch. Most of the guys had gone upstairs to bed or back to their apartments. Sam lived off campus too, but the flow of conversation wasn't about to be interrupted by something like overstaying our welcome.

I'd never gotten around to drinking anything that evening, and my fatigue from Rush and the last two years in general made it so I came across to him as myself. And Sam liked talking to that person enough that it was nearly daylight by the time I smoothed down my wrinkled skirt and announced that I should be getting back. I wrote my phone number on a half sheet of notebook paper and watched as he folded it carefully and placed it in his stuffed-to-the-gills wallet.

Sitting at breakfast with my sorority sisters, I got teased about my all-night liaison with a Delta Omega guy. Some of the girls who were a year older than me had known Sam for years and mused that they didn't see him as the womanizing, player type. And actually, we didn't even kiss that first night. So while physical intimacy was a major part of my relationship with Ryan for the wrong reasons, and a major part of my relationships with Nick and Jesse for slightly better reasons, Sam and I got off on a different foot entirely.

I rather liked the idea that we might be just friends. I'd had lots of guy friends throughout my life, and generally it worked out pretty well. And even though lately, whenever I thought of Ryan and Jesse, I did so unemotionally, like I'd been injected with an anesthetic, I wasn't stupid enough to think that the third time would be a charm. It would be better for everyone if we didn't let things go any further.

Still, when Sam called the next night and asked me if I wanted to hang out, I was, against my better judgment, excited. We had dinner at Dave's Italian Kitchen and then had some good laughs in the self-help department at Barnes & Noble.

He held my hand as we walked back to campus, and when we arrived at my house, I snuck him up to see my room. Alpha Tau's leadership was about forty years behind the rest of the country, and so technically our house did not allow men above the first floor. I had moved into a double with my friend Diana that quarter, and I slept on the top bunk. Diana wasn't home yet, so Sam climbed up like a monkey and pulled my bedcovers up to his chin. His eyes moved to the shelf where I kept my alarm clock and the round, '70s-style white-noise machine I used to block out street sounds. He laughed so loud I clamped my hand over his mouth.

"I don't believe this," he said.

"What? What is it?"

"I have never in my life met anyone with a white-noise machine. And not just any white-noise machine. The Sound Soother."

"You have one too? I get made fun of all the time."

"So do I."

"I've had it since I was a kid. I can't sleep without it."

"Me neither."

We continued laughing over this for a good five minutes. "Well, geez, that settles it. We must be soul mates."

The next week, Sam and I were chatting on telnet, the same campus system I'd used to converse with Ryan two years earlier. Midterms were coming up, and he typed that was about to pull an all-nighter studying physics. When he mentioned that he was planning to do a few lines of coke to get through it, I told him that he was very funny. But he stuck to the story, repeating that there was nothing wrong with a little cocaine, until he convinced me that I had just spent all night talking to a drug addict. I stormed downstairs to the common area, grumbling that with my mother and brother, I had all the druggies I needed in my life.

I interrupted a group of seniors watching *Party of Five* to demand why no one had told me that Sam was a straight-A on-the-homecoming-court student thanks to coke. They just laughed and said either he or I must be kidding. They couldn't think of a guy less likely to be involved with hard drugs than Sam. I slunk back upstairs and proceeded to ignore Sam's calls for two days.

Finally, I broke down and answered. "That was the lamest thing anyone's ever done to me," I said.

"It was stupid," he said. "I'm sorry."

"You should be. It's one thing to say it once as a joke, but you took it too far."

"I know."

"Drug addiction is not amusing to me." I suddenly felt like it was too much to go on and had the urge to hang up on him.

He sensed it and said, "This is why I never get anywhere with women. I don't have any social skills."

I softened. "Oh, come on. That's not true. You're a perfectly nice guy and a great conversationalist. But your sense of humor, it's…" Neither of us knew quite how to describe it. One part eccentric, one part standard guy wacky, one part twisted? "Whatever. Do not mess with my head like that ever again."

"I won't. I promise."

He was much better-behaved after that, pursuing me diligently. We went to the movies and to the decent ethnic restaurants in Evanston, which at the time were few and far between. Because he was so much like my twin, it had been easy for me talk to Sam since the first night we met, and I found myself revealing the cursory details of my past before we'd really done anything substantial physically. Since I wasn't heavily invested in whether this relationship would go anywhere, I had little to lose. If he thought I was nuts and bolted, so what?

Sam, in turn, told me about his family. He'd been born and raised in a middle-class Westchester suburb outside of New York City, and no one in four generations of his family had lived outside that area. His father was an accountant for a transportation company, his mother a secretary for a company that made adhesives.

Like me, Sam had grown up in the midst of perpetual chaos. He described his dad as good at male-bonding activities like Little League and barbecues, but emotionally absent. His mom was a loner who was ambivalent about family life, and his older sister, Gretchen, was very dramatic and usurped the little available attention of both parents. Their house shook with violent arguments from the time Sam was a toddler, and he coped by spending most of his time at friends' houses—learning how real people had conversations at the dinner table and how to dress for formal occasions. In the summers, he attended a boy's camp in New Hampshire, which he credited for every well-adjusted bone in his body.

His parents finally divorced when Sam was thirteen, and he was allowed to adopt what would become the love of his life, his border collie, Shea. When his mother moved him across town so that he could go to a better high school, Sam was furious and distraught at the idea of leaving his friends, and it was Shea he turned to for support.

In high school, he became an accomplished saxophone player and was accepted early decision to Northwestern when he was seventeen. College was great fun for him. He made a close group of friends in his dorm and used the fraternity for parties and associated drinking opportunities. His grades were excellent, his schedule well rounded. His one weakness was relationships.

I was in no position to be judgmental there, and Sam said he found me less intimidating than the other girls he'd dated at school. I did, however, often pull away from him for seemingly no reason. He stuck by me anyway and asked me to the Delta Omega winter formal. On a Saturday night right after Valentine's Day, he brought me roses, and we headed downtown to the Drake Hotel. Midway through the first slow dance, though, my knees buckled.

"Oh my God, are you okay?" Sam said.

The room was spinning. "I don't know," I said. "I feel kind of sick."

He helped me over to our seats at one of the round tables. I was suddenly feverish and shivered in my winter white strapless dress. Sam took off his suit jacket and placed it around my shoulders. "Let me get you some water."

I smiled weakly at the two girls sitting at the table, who were nodding in my direction sympathetically. Sam came back with a water glass and two Tylenol. I shook my head. "I think I might throw up."

"Let's go, then."

He came with me into the women's bathroom. I didn't vomit and instead huddled miserably in the corner. "I'm really sorry," I finally said. "This is your senior-year formal. You may never get to do this again."

He laughed softly. "Well, first of all, technically last year was my class's senior formal. And as for this year, this is the winter formal. The senior formal will be on some boat in the spring. We have two every year. No wonder we're always forking over more dues."

"Okay," I murmured and closed my eyes as I leaned against him.

"Let's get a cab and go back."

"That'll cost a fortune."

He stroked my head. "Don't worry about it."

It turned out that I had mono, and mono is one of those things that just has to run its course. My doctor at Evanston Hospital ordered uninterrupted rest, and so I temporarily moved to the sorority guest room downstairs. Sam visited me there almost every day, and, worried that I was contagious, I wouldn't kiss him. We just sat quietly together in the dark.

Every time I talked to my mother, she had a new plan for my recovery. I passed on all of her suggestions to my doctor and followed the ones it was possible to implement myself, but nothing worked. It was all I could do to keep up with my classes, and I was forced to resign from the Panhel Council. It was the first time in my life I'd quit anything, and I was knocked down with helplessness.

I was sick for most of the winter, but as the weather improved, so did I. Sam and I hung out regularly, eating pizza and Chinese takeout and lying side by side on his apartment's living-room floor with our heavy psych textbooks. He invited his college friends—most of whom had already graduated and were living in Chicago—over for dinner to meet me. I learned that they referred to all of Sam's love interests as "chicks." A girl in nursing school was "Nurse Chick." Another from Idaho was "Idaho Chick." My lucky moniker, however, was "Girlfriend Chick," and I knew that I had reached a place with Sam that no woman had dared venture before.

On one of those nights, with Peter Gabriel's *Us* album in the stereo, Sam and I had sex in his bedroom, on a mattress that was, in typical college-guy fashion, thrown on the floor with no supporting bed frame or box spring. I was again bewildered by the pain, but still way more comfortable with physical intimacy than other forms of intimacy. The next day, my dad visited from New York. We took him to brunch at Clark's, and Sam had the honor of being the first of my college boyfriends to meet my father.

"Thank you for taking such good care of Ally this winter," my dad said.

"You're welcome. She's very special."

Somehow, having the two most important men in my life at the same table gave more weight to our relationship than the previous evening's act. And back in my room at the house, I worried.

It didn't stop me for long, though, for in the last few years, I had proven myself an expert at stalwartly returning to the same dangerous situations. Soon, Sam and I were firmly entrenched in a relationship. This guy, who was two years my senior, was affectionate and stable and loyal, and even as I struggled with constant feelings of disconnectedness, there was something comforting in the fact that I'd finally found someone who had no intention of leaving me.

"You've been, like, a serial dater ever since Ryan," Jasmine observed.

I was insulted. "Believe it or not, I'm doing my best to have a long-term relationship."

"But don't you think that maybe you could just use a break? Be on your own for a while?"

"I'm perfectly fine on my own," I said. "But I keep meeting guys; what I can I say?" I chuckled.

Jasmine didn't smile.

In May, my mother came to visit me at school. I'd been at Northwestern for over two years, and it was only the second time she'd been there. In the sorority house, I was back to living upstairs, and so Mom got to stay in the little guest room I'd occupied during the winter months.

Hanging out with the girls—eating meals with us at the long, wooden tables, watching TV in the common room, and playing the piano and singing—my mother was having the most fun she'd had in years.

She was charismatic and charming with everyone, regaling the group with stories about how when I was a kid, I was as "strong as a bull," and the way my hands had developed was considered to be evolutionarily advanced. In return, the girls were more than happy talking to her about their classes and boyfriends. This mutual love-fest was a new phenomenon for me, as Mom had never shown much interest in my friends before.

She was not so positive about Sam. Sam and I had been to-gether five months, and in that time, he'd heard enough about my mother to conclude that he wanted to spend as little time with her as possible. When she visited, Sam was polite but cool. Because Mom felt rejected whenever someone wasn't brimming over with enthusiasm in her presence, she decided right away that she didn't like him.

After Mom and Sam initially met at brunch on Saturday, we were supposed to join up again for dinner. But Mom said she had a mi-graine and spent the afternoon sleeping, so I told Sam not to come over. A few hours later, she was chomping away happily on Chinese spare ribs in Alpha Tau's dining room.

"So how many times did she leave the house while she was here?" Sam asked me, after I'd put Mom in a cab to the airport.

"Once," I said. "Just to go to Osco."

Sam rolled his eyes. "What's she on now?"

"It's Percocet." Mom had apparently found a new doctor who spe-cialized in pain management for her headaches and was basically willing to prescribe my mother whatever her heart desired.

"Of course it is."

"She wasn't on my case that much. I think she always wanted to be in a sorority. All the girls really seemed to like her."

"It was the novelty factor," Sam said. "She was the center of atten-tion, and she could talk as much as she wanted."

There was something about Sam's condescending attitude toward Mom that bothered me. I was allowed to complain about her, but I didn't particularly appreciate it when other people did.

I'd realized that Sam had a critical side and was also a little self-ish. He wasn't used to being in a relationship and the give-and-take that went with it. He had a life of working late into the night on his honors theses and hanging out with friends downtown on the week-ends that he was quite happy with, and what I wanted to do had better fit in with his agenda.

I tried to act like I didn't care, but I bristled when Sam told me he didn't feel ready to introduce me to his family and when he brushed me aside, saying that I was acting like we'd been together five years instead of five months. Then, shortly before his graduation, Sam and I argued about his plans come September.

"I want to go to Germany," Sam announced one rainy afternoon as we were making broccoli-and-cheese soup in his kitchen. "There's a bioengineering lab at the University of Dresden I can apply to work in. I know enough German now that I can probably become fluent."

"How long are we talking?"

"I don't know, six months?"

"Six months!"

"It's not that long."

"What are you smoking? It's almost my entire senior year!"

"So what? I've been here five years already. It's not like I should be hanging around anyway."

"But what if I want you to hang around?"

"I'm finally graduating. It's time for me to get a life."

"Don't you want me to be part of that life?"

He let out this massive sigh. "Why do you have to make everything about you?"

I slammed one of the kitchen cabinets shut. "Fine, so this sum-mer is probably it for us, then. Because it's not like either of us has the money to jet-set back and forth from Germany. And what are you going to do for fun over there? You don't know anyone."

"I'll meet people."

"Right."

Sam's graduation arrived. His mother, father, and sister came out for it, and he reluctantly allowed me to meet them, but only because I would have had to miss the whole thing otherwise.

During the procession, Gretchen leaned over. "My brother doesn't even seem nervous," she whispered.

"Sam's been at this school a long time."

"He has always been pretty easygoing, I guess."

I almost laughed out loud. "Easygoing is not a word I'd use. He's had his whole life planned since he was twelve and it better not deviate one bit," I said.

"Wow. Seems like you know him better than I do."

I shrugged. "We're both in the dark."

When my own classes were over, I flew to Maryland. Why I felt the need to continually subject myself to the daily torture of being around my mother and brother, I didn't know. But no matter how much time I spent away, Gaithersburg still felt like home to me, and even though Dad was in New York and I had no safety net, I couldn't resist going back.

But once I got there, I was horribly claustrophobic. After I'd tried and failed to wake up Mom and Andy over a period of twelve hours, I took a cab to the metro and went downtown. I wandered around some of the bars and restaurants around Union Station and then stood on the corner of L Street and watched the cars drive past me, each one splashing a little more muddy water on my white sandals.

Possibly out of guilt for renting a small, one-bedroom apartment that I couldn't possibly stay in over vacations, my dad leased me a 1997 black Honda Civic, which I named Bullet. I was supposed to use it to get a job, but having come home at the end of June, nearly all the minimum wage labor in Montgomery County was taken. I interviewed at Bed, Bath, and Beyond but was told I was too short to stock the shelves properly. At the new Ruby Tuesday's, the manager said I didn't have enough experience as a waitress. I was so desperate I even went to an informational session on selling knives. But nothing panned out, and my friends were all too busy to see me more than once a week. I was stranded in the most depressing house on earth with nothing to do.

Mom had expressed passing interest in finally doing something with her paralegal degree, so I made her sit next to me as I typed her résumé. I tried to show her how to use Microsoft Office and the Internet too, since she would need them for any clerical job these days, but her attention span was ten minutes.

Every time I began to hope that we'd make enough progress on the job search to finally motivate her out of the house, another physical ailment would send her back to bed for days. Her pain-management doctor had her license revoked for writing improper prescriptions, and my mother and brother were on a mission to obtain the drugs they wanted through any means possible. Andy discovered the Internet for that purpose, and sadly, it was the only thing Mom would learn to use it for.

No relationship in the house was stable for more than a week at a time. I tried to get along with my brother, pushing him nicely but firmly to take Dad up on his offer to send him to NYU for college. One night, we stayed up late drinking beer in his bedroom and had a great talk about the necessity of separating physically and emotionally from Mom. I thought I'd gotten through to him, but the very next day, when I was talking to our grandmother on the phone in his room, Andy yanked the extension out of my hand and hung it up.

I stomped into the guest room and flopped down on the twin bed, where Mom's cat Magic was giving herself a bath. I scratched her belly, and she purred and rolled over so I could get a better angle. And then, with no warning, she hit me really hard on the wrist.

"Ow!" I yelped.

"What happened?" my mother asked, emerging from the cocoon of her room.

"Magic hit me," I tattled, as if the cat were the actual sibling Mom considered her to be.

"Well, did you provoke her?" Mom said.

It wasn't even worth answering. I walked downstairs, picked up the phone, and booked myself a train ticket to see Sam in Westchester.

My boyfriend took a couple of days off from his job at Barnes & Noble to hang out with me, but he acted like it was this gigantic sacrifice. He was frustrated that the University of Dresden hadn't yet committed to giving him a position in their bioengineering department, and he was surly toward me and, as I learned, his mother. Sam's mom might have been a little odd, but I was appalled at how he spoke to her. His anger at her simmered just underneath the surface, and a simple thing like a dirty tablecloth would send it shooting out and upward.

In Sam's room, where he'd spent most of his high-school career and all college summers, I found a stack of letters from his one former girlfriend. I wasn't jealous, merely intrigued, and the two of us read them aloud, sitting Indian style on the hardwood floor. The recollection of this romance, which hadn't really gone anywhere, seemed to depress Sam, so we shoved the letters back in the dresser drawer and decided to take the dog to the beach for a walk.

Shea sat in the front seat of Sam's light-blue Nissan, and I sat in the back, nearly wheezing from all the dog hair in the car. Glen Island Park was chilly and overcast, but Shea didn't seem to mind. She darted through the trees and sand with boundless energy. Sam chased and tackled her and covered her with kisses. I just stood there, my hands on my hips, observing the dynamics between my boyfriend and his mangy mutt.

"Oh my God," I said, over the song Sam was singing to Shea. "You love that dog more than me."

Both Sam and the dog looked up at me, bewildered. "What are you talking about?" Sam said.

"It's like I'm not even here."

"We're playing."

"I can see that."

"You're the one who doesn't want to be here."

"That's not true," I said. "But it would be nice if you didn't leave me to walk behind like a third wheel." As soon as it was out of my mouth, I couldn't believe I'd said it. How many times had I listened to my mother complain that when we went somewhere as a family, my father always took a kid in each hand and left her to fend for herself? Here I was airing the same grievance, and even worse, meaning it.

"You're strangling me, Ally," he said softly.

"I'm not doing anything," I said. "You're the one who snapped at me for taking a later train so I could see my dad first. Your mom cooks you all this food, and all you do is yell at her. You know, Mom always told me to pay close attention to how a boy treats his mother, because that's how he'll treat you someday."

"Go ahead and listen to her, hon. That'll take you far."

I was wearing shorts and a tank shirt and was covered in goose bumps, but my head felt like it was on fire. "You know what, this isn't working. I'm just going to go home."

"Now?"

"Now."

"You don't have to." Sam stood up and leashed Shea. He looked me up and down, as if to assess if I was bluffing. I wasn't. I was genuinely tired from having the same pointless conversations about dying relationships, and a large part of me was sorry that I'd even allowed myself to get involved with Sam.

We walked back to the car and silently got inside. "So are we breaking up?" he asked.

"It's probably for the best. I mean, you're going to Germany anyway."

He nodded but looked troubled as we drove back to his house. I wanted to leave right away, so I gathered my things and said good-bye to his mother. When Sam pulled up to the train station, he said, "I'll miss you."

"Me too."

The breakup only lasted for three weeks. It seemed that me walking away was exactly what Sam needed to prove that I wasn't as needy as he thought I was. He called me, but I didn't get back to him until he mailed me a mix CD of some of the songs from our time together and some that described how he was feeling now. As many relationship adventures as I'd had, no one had ever made me a genuine mix. Even my mother was impressed.

It wouldn't be summer at home without another medical procedure. I got colds all the time and had pretty bad allergies, and Mom's ear, nose, and throat doctor thought I should have my tonsils out. I was still terrified of surgery after what had happened the first time, and I never would have agreed to it had I known that Mom would abandon me on the day of the operation.

Complaining of diarrhea, she had Andy drive me to the hospital, and she wasn't there when I woke up in recovery unable to swallow. For the next twenty-four hours, I lay in my private room, alone, unable to be discharged because I couldn't choke water down and required an IV.

"I wish I didn't have to go back to Mom's house," I told Sam on the phone from the hospital.

"I don't blame you," he said. "But I'm glad you can talk again."

"It was ghastly."

"Yeah," he said. "And look, are you sure it was even necessary?"

A nurse came in and put a tray down in front of me. "What do you mean?" I asked.

"Well, like, it just seems that your mom is always pushing for some sort of medical intervention."

"She knows a lot about health stuff."

"All I'm saying is, have you heard of Munchausen by proxy?"

As a psychology major, I had. Munchausen by proxy syndrome is a type of child abuse that involves the exaggeration or fabrication of illnesses or symptoms by a caretaker—usually the mother. "Come on, Sam," I said. "Mom never poisoned me or anything like that. I've just always been kind of a sickly person."

"Maybe."

I had two weeks at home before I went back to school for my senior year, and Sam drove down to visit me. Mom had paid Andy a fortune to finish the basement, and Sam and I sat down there with the TV on. The U of Dresden opportunity was still not solidified, but Sam was going to Germany to see if he'd have better luck in person. He got on a plane overseas at the same time I got on one to Chicago.

For my senior year, I moved into a single in a dorm on campus. I thought I might graduate in a few months, so there was no point in getting an apartment for the year. The quarter started with the usual flurry of new classes and sorority activities, and on the weekends, Jasmine and I went clubbing downtown. But Sam did not allow me to forget him. In Germany, while he waited for the university department to give him something to do, Sam was backpacking around. He called me every night.

"What are the youth hostels like?" I asked.

"Exactly what you'd imagine," he said. "Dirty and loud. I haven't slept for a week and I'm starting to lose my shit."

"But there's so much history there," I said. "Even if it is the origin of Our People's demise."

"I don't know what I'm doing here. This isn't what I expected."

"Nothing's ever what we expect."

After another week, Sam started going to the university every day and found a place to stay with a German family in Dresden, but he was still miserable.

"What are you doing there?" he asked me constantly.

"The usual."

"I want to be doing the usual too."

One night, I answered my phone as I was returning from yet another friend's twenty-first birthday celebration. "This job is so boring and I can't talk to anyone here," Sam said, distraught. "And it's not just the language barrier. I miss you."

"All right, look, you gave it a chance," I said. "Just come home."

"Okay," he said, and he did.

Sam flew to New York and immediately back to Chicago. At first, he stayed with me in my tiny single and snuck into our dining hall for the bulk of his meals. He could have languished in his dashed postcollege dreams and squatted in my dorm room for months on end, but this was Sam we were talking about. He went right out and got a job interning at a stem cell research firm in Chicago. Days later, he moved into an apartment share in Andersonville with a fifty-five-year-old lesbian.

With my boyfriend back in town, it seemed to follow that I would want to stick around. But though Sam and I had evened out some and were as well suited as we'd ever been, I couldn't muster the enthusiasm for my current relationship that had ruled my mind for the last three years.

What Jasmine had said had finally penetrated. I was ready to be on my own for a while. I was conscious of the fact that my father had paid for my college education in full, and that I hadn't had to take out loans or work through school like many of my classmates. So, since I was finished with my graduation requirements, I decided to save Dad some money and leave Northwestern ahead of the rest of my class. My college record was respectable, nothing like my high-school one, but a transcript of mostly As and a handful of Bs every year got me a job as an account coordinator with a large advertising agency in New York City. I booked a one-way ticket and prepared to work sixteen hours a day and live in a six-hundred-square-foot apartment.

In the month before I left, I started running into Ryan several times a week—at Thai Sook Dee while I was having dinner with Sam, at the campus health club, and in Tech Auditorium's lecture hall where we shared an Intro to Buddhism class. Eyes averted. Hasty exit.

The coincidences piled up. And then, I finally got on the plane to start my new life in New York. Despite the variety of airlines offering service from Chicago to New York, and despite the number of flights scheduled all day every day, I came face-to-face with Ryan walking the other way down the aisle of my plane.

I was wearing my first real business suit and carried a new Kate Spade briefcase. Ryan and I stared at each other for a few long seconds, and then he gave me this little smile. He was so far away from me now that I couldn't even tell if it was real. It cemented my conviction to leave.

PART III

What is a force that binds the stars?
I wear this mask to hide my scars
What is the power that moves the tide
Never could find a place to hide
What moves the earth around the sun?
What could I do but run and run and run?
Afraid to love, afraid to fail
A mast without a sail.

—*Sting, "Ghost Story"*

I moved to New York City in the early spring of 1998. My one-bedroom apartment in the Gramercy neighborhood of midtown Manhattan cost $1,400 a month, which at the time was too much for me to afford. It wasn't unusual for twentysomethings to move in with complete strangers, and that's what I did. There was a service called Roommate Finders that people used to find suitable matches.

My first "suitable" match was a bleach-blond, deeply tanned girl from the South named Samantha. She turned out to be psycho, staying up all night decorating the walls with brown sponge paint and plotting how to seduce her older, married boss. We lived together for exactly one week, after which my father stepped in to extricate me.

I was accustomed to solving my own problems, obviously, but I was twenty-two years old and in over my head. Dad was reluctant, even though by New York standards he practically lived down the street.

There were a few shouting matches about my bad judgment. I regretted getting Dad involved, and in fact, I never did again when I was facing something genuinely significant or difficult. From that point on, I was only comfortable using my father as a sounding board for mundane issues related to work, like how I should ask my boss for a raise or a meaty project.

Samantha moved out, and I kept the apartment. My next roommate was a slightly more normal girl from Purchase named Carrie. She smoked a lot of weed and had a black cat that I adored. None of my friends had graduated yet, but Carrie had some friends in the city, so we went out to clubs in Alphabet City a lot. There were occasional Sunday nights when I got home at four o'clock only to leave for work at eight thirty. During the rest of the workweek, we ate cold cereal in front of the TV and watched *Dawson's Creek* and *Felicity*.

After a few months of living in New York City, I returned to Evanston for my official graduation from Northwestern. I felt worldly compared to my fellow seniors. I didn't have much time to reflect on what this event meant in the context of my life, because my whole immediate family attended and was a nightmare come to life. My mother was too cold, the graduation festivities were too spread out, and my father and brother were "rude and abusive" to her. After two days, I happily went back to New York.

My job as an account coordinator for the global advertising firm McCann Erickson was walking distance from the apartment. At the beginning, the work was okay. Although I didn't relish using my $100,000 education to fax reporters and process expense reports, I enjoyed researching new health conditions and teaching my senior colleagues how to use the Internet. But my boss, Catrina, a twenty-six-year-old account supervisor who seemed impossibly old and experienced to me, the youngest person on staff, decided pretty early on that she couldn't stand me. In meetings, her gaze was coolly critical, and she made happy-hour plans with the rest of our team behind my back—leaving me sitting in the office at six in the evening alone.

One fall afternoon after I had been at McCann for six months, she appeared in front of my desk, which was in the hallway. "Ally, can I see you in my office a minute?"

Trotting behind her warily, I said, "Sure."

"Look, I think it's only fair that I let you know that your career is self-destructing."

My eyes widened. In twenty-two years, I had not been told I sucked that badly at something related to school or work.

Catrina had a doughy face with features that looked smeared on. She twisted on a smile that showed one or two teeth. "The other girls on the team don't like you. They think you're a know-it-all."

"Really?" I whispered.

She said some other things, but I was incapable of hearing them. There was a train in my head. I grabbed my notebook and headed for the elevator. I frantically pushed buttons until I landed in the lobby, where I collapsed on the street and forced myself to breathe. All I could think was: Catrina hadn't criticized my work after all. She hated my personality. Just like Ryan. Just like my mother.

The next day, I went back to work and talked to my HR rep. But while she seemed genuinely committed to resolving the situation between Catrina and me, I decided that I had to get away. It didn't occur to me to do something to change the dynamic. I couldn't bear to be in the same space with my flaws, so for the first time in my life, I quit something voluntarily.

I wasn't unemployed for long. My online sleuthing skills were in high demand, and two senior colleagues who were leaving McCann for better opportunities competed to take me with them. I accepted an offer doing audience research for a blood pressure medication at another advertising giant, DDB Worldwide.

My group head was a little unhinged, but, under the tutelage of an older coworker, Tamika, I learned to look and act in ways that

pleased her. I dressed in designer business casual like a VP and became a skilled conversationalist in power-player interests from yoga
to martinis.

"You know," Tamika said one afternoon. "You haven't left that
cube once all day. No one even knows you're in here."

"I'm earning my $30,000 salary," I replied. "I just finished my
third market analysis, and it's good."

"Ally, no one cares," she said. "The whole senior team is at Star-
bucks."

"But I can do another one."

"I'm sure you can, but right now you need to go downstairs and
talk to the people who need to pay attention to your work."

"I don't know what to say."

"Find out what they want to hear, and say that. Talk about your
work like it's going to solve all their problems."

"I'm scared."

"You are allowed to be scared for sixty more seconds," Tamika
said. "And then it's over. People who act intimidated don't get pro-
moted."

I followed Tamika out of our cube farm, mustering a bright smile
and a belief that I was the hottest new upstart in the whole place. I
didn't get any more market analyses done that day, and Tamika was
right—no one cared.

I continued to live it up in Manhattan. When our lease was up,
Carrie moved out, and a same-aged coworker from DDB joined me in
Gramercy. Liz and I celebrated our new relationship with a huge party. We ate out at a new restaurant every night and hung out with other
new grads in the Upper East Side apartment complex, Normandy
Court. It was known as "Dormandy Court" because everyone who
lived there was under the age of thirty.

I also went on a series of first dates, because why not? Sam was in
Chicago, and we had decided to give seeing other people a go. But
nothing really clicked, and as Sam came to visit me more and more,
the dating experiment petered out.

Jasmine moved back to New York and started working at *People* magazine. Under the shadow of the Y2K threat, she, Liz, Sam, and our other friends and I celebrated New Year's Eve, 1999, high in the office tower adjacent to where they dropped the Ball.

By the time we figured out nothing was going to happen with Y2K, we were too drunk to care. We crossed the Brooklyn Bridge on foot amid revelry from a million other partiers and landed in an all-night diner in Brooklyn Heights.

The new century was certainly celebrated in style, and my resolutions were appropriately ambitious. The biggest development was that I'd be living on my own. I rented a one-bedroom apartment in Astoria, Queens, a short subway ride from my office. The building was down the street from a famous Greek restaurant, from which one could hear the shouts of "Opa!" and smell the flaming cheese saganaki late into the still winter nights.

Of course, I needed a pet to go with my new apartment, so I went to the animal shelter in Brooklyn and selected a female calico that was so terrified she didn't move. I put her in a carrier, took her home on the train, and named her Adrienne.

After the solo apartment and the cat, I wanted to lose the twenty pounds I had put on while eating five thousand calories of desserts every day, and I wanted to move to the newly formed digital marketing group within DDB. The team was working on the first major corporate website for a consumer-goods giant, and I wanted in on the action. And finally, I wanted to get Andy out of our mother's house.

At least once a week, my mother called, furious or hysterical (or both) about some issue related to Andy. He was stealing from her. He had tried to kill her. The police had come to the house and threatened him. As the situation escalated, I couldn't help feeling a bit vindicated. After all, all my life my mother had made no secret of the fact that my brother was her favorite. But I was growing a bit weary of all the drama, and also a bit fearful that I would soon get a call from the Gaithersburg Police Department. Except, instead of just my mother being dead, my brother would be dead too.

Andy moved out of his room on the second floor and into the basement, which he had refurbished so that he could launch an on-line bookselling endeavor. Although my brother had only a GED to show for his years of school and could only be bothered to take a few classes here and there at the local community college, his business was a modest success. But he and my mother were both taking more and more prescription drugs, mainly to sleep, and at times it didn't seem like either of them was sane.

"We had a little problem here," Mom said, almost seductively, on the phone one day when I was walking to Jenny Craig after work.

"What now?"

"I had a growth on my arm, about the size of a tennis ball," she informed me. "I didn't want to go to the ER, so Andy cut it off."

"He what?" I nearly screamed. Several pairs of eyes in the Jenny Craig lobby turned to look at me sympathetically. Family chaos was not good for weight loss.

"He took a knife and some alcohol and lanced it."

"Jesus."

"But now it won't stop bleeding."

I sighed. "Mom, you have to go to the ER."

Andy still had health insurance through my father, but Mom didn't, and she was burning through her mother's money with alarming speed. Mom might not have wanted to go to the ER this time, but she went to a psychiatrist and spent hundreds of dollars on drugs every week.

Mom and Andy needed a change in dynamic immediately, so I relented and told my brother he could visit me in New York. Dad and I had said he couldn't come unless he agreed to move out of Mom's house and go to school, but I felt so sorry for him. He was barely twenty-one years old, with no meaningful relationships and no education. He slept all the time, and when he was awake, he managed to smoke a pack of cigarettes every day. His life seemed doomed.

Andy rode the train up. I took him to dinner and *Saturday Night Live*, and he stayed overnight at my apartment. It was a pleasant weekend, one of the few times I can remember when my brother and I had an extended period of normal interaction. And when he went home, I felt the familiar sensation of guilt, like I was abandoning him all over again.

He did move out, though. After Mom called the police on him for the third time, Andy decided he'd had enough. Dad finally gave him the money in Andy's college fund, and Andy used it to lease a studio apartment in Germantown.

But his life didn't change much, and I felt something akin to grief. I wasn't sure exactly what was wrong with Andy these days: I'd heard everything from chronic depression to sleep disorder to drug addiction. It might have been none of the above or all of the above. I did know that he was undisciplined. Nothing I said motivated him. He wanted to blame our parents for everything and felt entitled to this wonderful life without putting any effort into it. He was smart and charismatic, and his existence seemed to be an utter waste of potential. I kept telling myself that at least he was free of our mother.

Months after I won a spot on DDB's digital marketing team and had dropped most of my graduation-induced weight, Sam learned that he had been accepted to a bioengineering Ph.D. program at the State University of New York at Stony Brook. In the fall, he would be moving to eastern Long Island, and I had to decide if I wanted to go with him.

I didn't give much thought to this. By the time I was twenty-four, I'd been changing my living situation every year for six years, and moving in together seemed like the next logical step in our relationship. It was slightly problematic that I associated Long Island with Ryan, but I was won over by being a short drive from one of the most beautiful beaches on the East Coast. The move did mean, however, that I'd have to get a new job. Commuting fifty miles to and from the city every day was not something anyone wanted to do.

With a loan from his mom, Sam bought a cute two-bedroom condo in Smithtown. Before Adrienne and I moved in in late 2000,

I searched for a job in an internal advertising department at a company in Long Island. I didn't have a lot of choices. There were exactly three large companies on the island that would hire someone with my experience, and none had posted openings. I relied on copying names and numbers off websites and contacting those people for advice about the local marketing community. The strategy worked. I hit it off so well with one guy that he convinced his boss to create a position for me at the barcode scanning company Symbol Technologies.

Again, my life changed radically in a short period of time, yet my attention was far away from what was happening to me. Now that my brother was out of the house, my mother gripped me tighter through the miles.

"How long do you intend to live there?" she asked me, of Long Island.

"Sam's going to be in grad school for three more years."

I heard her sigh through the phone. "So I guess that's it for you two, then."

"What do you mean?"

"You're going to get married."

In the parking lot at Symbol, I switched off the ignition. Someone had decorated the building entrance for Valentine's Day, but it had snowed the previous night and the crepe hearts looked damp, the red tinsel weighted down. "I'm twenty-four, Mom. I'm not marrying anyone."

"I always thought you'd come back to Maryland after college."

"Why?"

"Because your mother is here, for one," she scoffed. "You obviously have no interest in a close relationship with me."

The parking lot was starting to fill up. A fellow employee pulled in next to me. He honked and gestured that I was over the line. "Mom, I have to go to work."

"Darcy and I have been getting together a lot."

Darcy still lived across the street. Her children were now grown as well. "That's great," I said. "How's she doing?"

"She comes over and gets me out of bed. We are going to a temp office tomorrow. I could really use your help revising my résumé. I was telling Darcy how you talked yourself into a job out there."

Even though Mom was always saying she wanted go to back to work, the prospect still invoked a feeling of pleasant lightness in my chest. "Send me what we did before and I'll try my best," I said.

I did manage to draft an impressive-sounding résumé for a fifty-five-year-old woman who had been out of the workforce for nearly a decade and needed a menagerie of pills to get anywhere on time. And Mom and Darcy did go to the temporary-employment office. Mom went on one or two jobs, but she found tasks involving a computer overwhelming—which in 2001 was everything.

Darcy was one for projects. She had been my Girl Scout troop leader once and still actively volunteered in her church. But after one too many despondent calls from my mother in the middle of the night, Darcy quit this particular project. Who could blame her, really?

After hanging up with Darcy, Mom called me five times. I was talking to Liz so I ignored the first several attempts. When I finally picked up, Mom sobbed that everyone in her life had left her and that she'd be dead in the morning.

Feeling a mix of exasperation and terror, I got in the car and drove down to Maryland. By then, the house was such a disaster—reeking of her cats and still covered with boxes piled high to every ceiling—that I stayed in a Hampton Inn a few miles away.

I accompanied my mother to a new therapist and helped her assemble several business outfits for interviews. I held her attention for a full hour while I patiently explained how to do a mail merge in the new Microsoft Word. Cheered, Mom talked about becoming an interior designer. She made appointments with three temp firms. "And hey," she said gleefully. "Maybe I'll learn sign language. I've heard it can come in handy!"

"That's great, Mom," I said. "I'm sure Andy would appreciate that one."

She pledged to detox and even promised to call my grandparents in California, from whom she'd been estranged for years. Feeling high from another mission accomplished, I pulled out of the driveway with Bruce Springsteen crooning on the radio. I wasn't even at the Delaware border before my mother lost her will to do any of this and returned to bed.

The summer of 2001 was, on paper, glorious. Sam and I were twenty-seven and twenty-five years old. We were on sensible life paths and spent every weekend driving up to Cape Cod or Martha's Vineyard or lying out at the Fire Island National Seashore. We ate exotic meals in the city with Liz, her boyfriend John, Jasmine, and other friends. We enjoyed a parade of visitors and started attending the weddings of the first of our childhood and college friends.

Like all of my postgraduation work experiences, the job at Symbol was stressful. I had learned the game from Tamika at DDB, but I now played it so well I annoyed myself. I still longed for the days when success was based on merit, but in a huge company with a lot of bureaucracy and politics, Tamika's advice was more relevant than ever. Most people didn't care what happened and just wanted to go home.

Inside my head, I couldn't help railing against developments that didn't make any sense. When my team went to Atlanta to create a new campaign for a customer that loathed us, I gave myself a headache so severe that the words on my laptop screen were blurring.

As the summer marched on, I grew more and more tired. It wasn't unusual for me to come home from work at five thirty and fall asleep on the couch, waking up in enough time to eat some cold spaghetti, watch *The Sopranos*, and do a little work on my new novel about the inner lives of teen celebrities.

But I couldn't seem to muster up much passion about anything—good or bad. I didn't care about sex at all, which pissed off Sam, of course. He demanded that I return to therapy.

I dutifully sat in the office, which was the den in my counselor's house. Although my therapist was a man, the room had clearly been decorated by a woman. The pastel tones were intended to calm the most anxious of patients, and the tasteful fake floral arrangements were posed in exactly the right places. From my position in a mauve velour armchair, I saw Dr. Kagan's kids returning from school.

"How are you feeling about your job?" he asked me.

"I'm a corporate whore," I said nonchalantly. "A complete sellout."

"And this doesn't bother you?"

"Sometimes it really does. The rest of the time I don't think about it."

"Don't think about it or won't think about it?"

I shrugged. "Both?"

We paused as an ambulance shrieked down the residential road. "Sounds like the city," Dr. Kagan mused.

"Sam thinks I don't care about him," I offered. "And he says my new novel is like reading a medical journal."

"And what do you think about that?"

"It's not that I don't care, exactly. I want to have a good relationship, and I want to be a good writer. It's just that this, I don't know, this indifference, it feels better."

"Have you heard of Masters and Johnson?"

"Yeah. I was a psych major in college."

"They developed a program called sensate focus. The basic idea is that a couple limits their sexual contact for a while. I'll give you and Sam some specific exercises to touch each other in certain ways. The focus is off sex in the traditional sense, so you'll get back in touch with your senses and hopefully regain some of your intimacy."

I nodded and squinted at a handout Dr. Kagan passed across the coffee table. "Verbal feedback is limited unless you're uncomfortable or in pain. Do not try to elicit a sexual response," I repeated, admittedly in a tone reminiscent of a flight attendant's pre-takeoff instructions.

But Sam was on board that flight, so sensate focus it was. It felt a little silly sometimes, but I was committed to giving it my best effort. Prompted by my grandfather, who was convinced he had known my grandmother in a past life in Egypt thousands of years ago, I started reading books on the occult to see if some spirituality would help. The idea of reincarnation wasn't foreign to me—I had written a novel about soul mates after all, and Jasmine had taught me about tarot cards in college. But I grew curious about the possibilities. I also loved *The Matrix* movies, fascinated by the idea that there could be another world just on the edge of consciousness, the potentially "real" reality.

I took hikes around the more picturesque areas of Long Island by myself, including the lush wine country of the North Shore and the endless stretch of white beaches of the Hamptons. I'd play classical music through my headphones, grasping for the one passage that would make me think of angels or ancient people. Every now and then, I felt like I was standing at the edge of time, like I'd caught hold of a fragment of another life, an alternative existence that was as clear to me as any memory and as real as any daily experience. In that place, my mind was quiet and my soul danced. But then I'd come home, and things would go back to normal. I was in a bubble, and everything came through my senses muted.

It was in this state of mind that I answered my phone at 8:50 a.m. on September 11, 2001. My colleague Judy told me that not a single person had dialed in to our scheduled nine o'clock webinar on content marketing. I let out a giant sigh of irritation when another colleague showed up at my cube and told me to turn on the TV.

My team and I watched in dumb horror as a second plane crashed into the World Trade Center just after nine. The buildings fell minutes later—we could see the smoke from fifty miles away. All of the cell-phone towers in New York City were down, and there was no way of reaching my dad and friends for several hours. Our office closed, and not knowing what to do with myself, I walked to the empty gym and walked silently, heavy-footed, on the treadmill.

Eventually, Sam and I found our way to the house of a graduate-school friend, where we watched CNN and were bombarded with the same gruesome images over and over. No one talked much. It was as if we had this vague but pervasive sense of unease that the future was now uncertain and none of us were safe.

Through the next several days, we all stumbled along, most of us not having the right to claim genuine grief. Being in New York, everyone in my immediate circle knew someone who had died—acquaintances who worked in the Towers and acquaintances who were first responders mostly—and yet the tragedy remained in the abstract.

I found myself thinking about the people in their twenties, like me—all those bond traders who were literally worked to death and never had a chance to step out of those buildings and see the world, find something they loved to do. Their existence consisted of sleepless nights in front of a screen, empty Styrofoam coffee cups, and a permanent resting place of melted steel columns and crushed ceilings. I wanted to love my own life more because they had sacrificed theirs. Yet no matter how hard I tried, I couldn't seem to make the connection.

As the whole world waited warily to see if another attack was going to happen, my mother was in her element.

"They may have hit the Pentagon, but that wasn't the plan," she insisted one night on the phone. "I'm sure they wanted to take out all of Washington. I always said that in a terrorist attack we'd be the first to go."

"DC will be fine," I said. "I don't know about New York, though." Not only was the cleanup downtown taking weeks, but the rest of Manhattan was like a ghost town. We'd go in for dinner and find no people on the streets and no traffic on the roads, and we would end up leaving early. Three thousand people may have died in September, but eight million residents of New York City had not recovered.

"You wait and see," Mom said. "This is just the beginning."

She sounded almost glad about it. My mother was the ultimate example of misery loves company, in fact welcoming it with open arms and asking it to stay the weekend. I listened to her drone on for a while about the end of modern civilization while I absently brushed a mat out of Adrienne's fur.

Mom was wrong, thankfully. For the most part, the crisis of 9/11 was limited to that day. And I was back to being doped into a state of apathy, more or less content with my usually nice boyfriend and our gradually improving intimacy, fun but not superclose group of post-college friends, paycheck-delivering job, clean house, and cat.

In the recesses of my mind, I wondered what my future would bring: would I be someone's wife or someone's mother; would I publish a novel, become an advertising director? The mountain of decisions I'd have to scale to arrive at the answers seemed insurmountable.

In the late winter of 2002, I submitted my novel about a clique of young celebrities, called *Idol Makers*, to a handful of literary agents. I was genuinely ecstatic when a well-known young-adult-fiction agent, Jason Tremain, called me immediately and asked to take me on as a client. I took the Long Island Rail Road into Manhattan to meet him for lunch at the Union Square Cafe.

A flamboyant hipster in his fifties, Jason had kept his cashmere scarf on inside the restaurant and looked good doing it. I was barely out of my rain-soaked jacket when he hugged me like a long, lost friend. "Allison Golden, my latest discovery!"

"It's really great to meet you, Jason."

He looked me over. "You are so young!"

I placed my umbrella in the stand in the vestibule. Jason took my hand and guided me to a table by one of the windows, pointing out the Cafe's obscure art and neo-classical Judy Rifka murals. The décor of the Cafe was purposefully minimalist and managed to look just the right amount of worn. As we looked at the outrageously expensive menus, I wondered who was going to pay.

Jason leaned close to me and I smelled Altoids. "My assistant reads hundreds of query letters and fifty manuscripts a week. She called me at home to make sure I saw *Idol Makers* right away."

"I'm so glad you both liked it. The research was fun. Did I tell you I talked to some actual teen celebrities?"

"It shows," he said enthusiastically. "The dialogue is spot-on. Ally, if you'll have me, I have a target list of editors already. I think I can get an offer next week."

"Seriously?"

"Yes!" Jason said. The waiter arrived with two glasses of champagne from the long, mahogany bar, which we toasted. "Now listen, normally I make my new authors do revisions prior to submission, but this is hot. In fact, I want to start talking about your next book. Do you want to do a sequel or something completely new?"

Holy cow. Nearly overnight, it appeared that my career was about to veer in a new direction. Someone thought my work was good. In his mind, I was no longer lumped with the jobless wannabes who think they should be given a Pulitzer because they tried to write a book.

While *Idol Makers* was on submission to editors, a friend of a friend who worked at Showtime got ahold of the manuscript and said her boss wanted to consider the material for a series. "This is unbelievable!" Jason crowed. "But not really. I tell you, Ally, the dialogue..."

Jason was so confident, I thought the sale of *Idol Makers* was as good as done. But ten editors passed and Jason started to lose steam. "I've heard that new novelists have to get rejected like a hundred times," I said.

"Not my novelists," he said grimly. " I am rarely wrong, but I may have been in this case."

Showtime didn't make a series either. This was especially unfortunate, since barely a year later HBO came out with a new show called *Entourage* that had much of the same plot and tone—and it was a huge hit.

"It's never going to happen," I told Sam as we ate dinner in Port Jefferson at our favorite pasta place. It was a rare occasion that I didn't bother about my weight, because I knew that the black lobster ravioli was worth every calorie.

"Come on, yes it will," he said. "Some people write a dozen books before one gets published."

"I know, but I just have this feeling that it's over."

"It might be over for *Idol Makers*, but not for you as a writer. Remember what Jason said. You have to write for yourself. Everyone loves celebrities, celebrities are cool, but you don't know that world. What world do you know?"

Huh. This was interesting, because as my weeks-old fiction-writing career was tanking, my advertising career was doing the opposite. At Symbol, I'd had the opportunity to take the Dale Carnegie course and had mastered skills that had eluded me during my first few years of working. Now that I knew better how to focus on the things that mattered to me AND to other people, my job was going better than ever. Maybe I should write a book for high achievers dumped into nonsensical Corporate America. It was, after all, the one book I wished I had.

My conscientiousness had always been a gift from God for all I'd had to put up with. I spent the remainder of the year researching and interviewing for, and then writing, the book that would eventually be called *Suit Yourself*. I still had a full-time job, so my little side project required that I work a lot of late nights and weekends.

Nonfiction was a new world for me that proved much easier to navigate. There were twists and turns for sure, including a publisher bankruptcy and a midprocess agent switch, but none of the setbacks ever convinced me that *Suit Yourself* wouldn't see the light of day.

On a rare Saturday when I wasn't tied to my computer, Sam and I went to the animal shelter on Long Island's South Shore and adopted a yippy little kitten. Our vet had told us that matriarch Adrienne would do better with a baby than an adult cat, and Sam and I liked the idea of raising a pet together.

As for the kitten himself, he seemed to recognize Sam instantly. He only had eyes for my boyfriend, ignoring all the little kids who were trying to pick him up. He meowed so loudly when Sam put him down that there was no way we were leaving that building without him.

Sam and I cleverly named the cat Pauly. We liked the *Rocky* films, in which character Paulie was character Adrienne's brother.

I was diligently typing away on the edits to *Suit Yourself* when Sam came home from the vet. He showed me the kitten's new collar. "You spelled his name wrong," I said.

"What? No I didn't."

"It's supposed to be Pauly with a 'Y.'"

"Um, no," Sam said. "See for yourself. Look on IMDB."

I returned to my chapter on diplomacy. We never would agree on the spelling of the cat's name, but Sam and I had reached a new phase in our relationship. We had two cats and a mortgage. The late twenties and everything they entailed were creeping up on us.

Around this time, Mom decided she would visit me in New York. She now had four cats herself and related better to felines than she did to humans. So it made sense that she wanted to meet Pauly, who to Mom was as important as a full-blooded grandchild.

I picked her up from Islip Airport on a summer day so oppressive that the air shimmered. Although she distracted me so much while I was driving that I knocked one of the headlights off our new Saturn, Mom's trip started off better than expected. She wanted to go to the beach, an activity that was always fine by me. All her life she'd wanted to live near the ocean, and now I did.

Mom didn't have a bathing suit, so she borrowed one of mine. It was gratifying as all hell that we now wore the same size. Since Mom was borderline anorexic, and I was chunky (her word), this had never happened before despite us being roughly the same height. It was a cloudless day with a light breeze and calm waves. During the few hours we splashed around together, I recalled the day we'd spent on this exact beach with Dad almost a quarter century ago.

Mom was pleased with the outing too. "When you were growing up, I always looked forward to you being in your twenties and finally pleasant."

"I'm glad you're happy, Mom."

Then, when Mom was about to leave, I asked her if she could ship me her Rosenthal china set. She'd mentioned that she hadn't used the dishes in over ten years, and Sam and I were planning to host our first formal Thanksgiving. After initially agreeing, she now had a change of heart.

"I think I'd better sell it instead," she said. "It's worth a fortune, and I need the money."

"It's not worth that much. I looked online."

"It might be a blessing in disguise, Ace. I haven't seen my pattern anywhere in years. It's definitely closed stock, so you couldn't replace a broken plate or add to the collection. It's much better to have something modern that's still open stock."

"But Grandma gave it to you," I said. "It's kind of like an heirloom, and you said I could have it."

"It's priceless, and I could make lots of money from it."

"It's not…" I got up from the couch and stomped into the hallway. "Forget it."

Mom followed me. "I didn't anticipate these money problems."

"Money problems happen when you stockpile drugs from the Internet and order a hundred pairs of shoes in a year and don't work," I said.

"I can't work."

"You won't work."

"How about giving me a break!" she said. "You've got it good, Ally. You were born with a silver spoon in your mouth and have wanted for nothing."

I picked up my copy of the sci-fi masterpiece *Ender's Game* and thumbed through it, glaring at her. "I want for a lot of things, but seeing as I'll never get them from you, I'll settle for the china."

"I'm sorry I can't give you what you think you deserve. Let's remember that all your life, things have been easy," she said. "I worked for years and handed the money over to you so you could have everything you wanted."

If I wasn't so angry, I might have marveled at my mother's ability to turn things around so that a broken promise on her part was now about me being a spoiled brat. "Are you packed?" I said. "We should probably go."

"Your attitude and greed are unbelievable," she went on. "I think I've been extremely generous with my love, time, money, emotional support, respect, all of it. You realize that I have no one to help me at all. No parents, no siblings, no husband, and no health insurance. I'd die if I had to depend on the state or you to keep me going."

This was ordinarily the place where, in my head, I'd wrestle with whether she was right or wrong about me. I'd reason with her, try to convince her that I had no desire to see her go broke over some porcelain plates. I'd tell her that I would step in if she ran out of money, but that she really needed to curtail her own spending in order to stretch her inheritance. But I was tired. With Mom, I was always the bad guy, and that would never change.

Pocketbook in hand, she opened the front door. "I'll never live up to your expectations, and I'm done trying."

"Me too," I said.

I loaded her bag into the trunk, and we drove to the airport in silence.

In January of 2003, Sam and I got engaged. I had a feeling it was coming, but Sam did a spectacular job of planning a scavenger hunt with the first clue starting at our condo and the final clue culminating on a blustery stretch of beach at Robert Moses State Park. The one-carat round diamond in a channel setting of yellow gold was exactly what I would have chosen myself, and the day after Sam put the ring on my finger, we got busy planning our 2004 wedding.

Families normally grow closer together during times like this. In our case, though, the level of desired involvement depended on the individual. Sam's mom was pretty checked out. My father didn't want me to repeat his mistakes. For our own sanity, we wanted to involve my mother as little as possible. So Sam's dad, Richard, and his long-term girlfriend, Beatrice, became our allies in the process. They wanted to invite a bunch of people to the wedding, so they had a vested interest in making sure the affair was to their liking.

Early on, we agreed to split the not-small cost of a New York wedding three ways. My dad, who was only having a few people, would pay a third as father of the bride. Rich would pay another third, and Sam and I would pay the final third ourselves.

Rich and Bea were wonderful about driving with us all over the New York metro area to select a venue. Having just planned a wedding for Sam's sister, Gretchen, they were pros. As we were dutifully led around banquet halls in five different counties in New York and Connecticut, Rich and Bea always knew when a dance floor would be too small or hotel accommodations too expensive for out-of-town guests.

By the spring, we had selected a large bed-and-breakfast resort at the foothills of the Berkshire Mountains. Called Troutbeck, the resort was homey and rustic but big enough to hold a wedding for 150 people and house the whole bridal party in quaint B-and-B-style rooms on the property. We chose a date in March and prepared for a year of driving two hours in each direction to choose food, flowers, music, photography, video, and even a local Jewish rabbi to marry us.

Since a wedding was something to organize, I had a blast attending to every detail, from the custom-designed invitations to the CDs we'd give out as favors. Sam's mom unexpectedly threw us an engagement party at our condo in Long Island, and it was the first time my parents had been together in the same place in eight years.

Naturally, this made the occasion more about my mother and her discomfort than the fact that Sam and I were getting married. She sat on our blue velvet couch in a beige silk ensemble and did not move. Our friends and Sam's relatives took turns approaching her like she was a queen seated on a throne in a presence chamber.

"Mrs. Golden, it's so nice to see you," said Liz.

"Thank you. I very nearly didn't make it."

"Did you fly from Reagan?"

"BWI," said my mother. "Reagan might be the worst airport on the planet."

"They have a good sushi place there," Liz said.

"I wouldn't know."

There were sixty people at the engagement party, so I, of course, had to make the rounds. Mom alternated glaring at me and Dad, who had come with his girlfriend Carol and left after an hour. Several guests were still hanging around when Mom stood up and announced that she was going to take a nap in the guest room.

She padded back into the living room about eight o'clock and stood in front of Sam and me in a pair of navy blue Victoria's Secret pajamas. "Hey Mom, there's sweet and sour chicken and rice in the fridge if you want it," I said.

"You had dinner already?"

"We didn't know what time you were getting up."

"I guess I should be used to it. This whole thing is being done without me." As Mom turned toward the kitchen, Sam rolled his eyes. "I think I'll catch an earlier flight tomorrow. If I'd wanted to be ignored, I could have stayed in Maryland."

I took the bait. I couldn't help myself. "How can you possibly say you were ignored? Every time I looked over there a new person was talking to you."

"I don't fit in," she said. "Maybe I shouldn't come to the wedding."

"That's up to you," I said. "But we would like for you to be there."

"I see your brother didn't bother to show," she pointed out. Andy had been invited to the engagement party, but I just assumed he'd been short on cash and tolerance for our mother. Dad promised me that he would make sure my brother came to the wedding outfitted in the appropriate attire. He would also take care of helping my elderly grandparents travel from California.

Mom left the next morning on her designated flight, and the next several months passed quickly. Contracts were delivered, roles were assigned. Liz, who had just gotten engaged herself, would be my maid of honor. Tina, Jasmine, and Gretchen would be my bridesmaids. My college friend Pete was one of Sam's groomsmen and Andy one of his ushers.

Our wedding colors were powder blue and white, our flowers pastel roses and hydrangeas. We'd write our own vows and splurge on a soul band instead of a cheesy DJ. We gleefully zipped around Macy's and Crate and Barrel with the registry scanner and booked a two-week honeymoon in Australia and New Zealand. Sam and I made all the decisions, and as our tastes were remarkably similar, there were few disagreements.

In an effort to appease Mom after the engagement party, I invited her to come up and help me shop for my gown. Thanks to her strong opinions about what did and did not look good on me, the process didn't take very long. My mother had been telling me my arms were fat since I was nine years old, so it was no surprise that a strapless gown was out of the question.

We went to two stores and spent an afternoon looking at dresses, eventually selecting a long-sleeved, beaded gown with a sweetheart neckline and A-line bodice. While she did whine about being tired and not feeling well, Mom seemed to enjoy a temporary journey into the "my daughter is getting married" fantasy. I even managed to get her excited about her own gown. But six months out, it was anyone's guess whether Mom would physically appear at the wedding.

At the end of January, Liz threw me an exquisite bridal shower at the King's Carriage House on the Upper East Side of Manhattan. We followed up our afternoon of tea sandwiches and scones with a bachelorette party of dinner and karaoke. It was a glorious weekend, made all the more glorious by the fact that Mom wasn't there to cause drama.

Two weeks later, Sam and five of his best friends from all over the country headed to Miami for the bachelor party. Then suddenly it was March, and the wedding was imminent. I spent way too many work hours on my planning site at TheKnot.com making last-minute budget calculations and jiggering with the seating chart.

By the time the Golden/Roth wedding contingent headed up-state for the rehearsal dinner, Rich, Bea, and Liz knew what we were dealing with when it came to my mother and graciously volunteered to shield me until the wedding was over.

Mom decided to come, but her trip was not without incident. First, she missed her plane and had to be rerouted. Next, she threw a fit when she found out I'd be getting dressed for the wedding with my bridesmaids—and no one else. And finally, she got into a fight with Andy on their way to the rehearsal dinner. They could have been arguing about anything, but Andy had brought his girlfriend Luane to New York. This made for a toxic triangle.

In any case, Andy got so mad at her that he opened the passenger door of his rental car and demanded Mom get out. Then, he and Luane drove away. My brother actually abandoned our mother on a country road in the middle of nowhere. Mom miraculously had cell reception and called Bea.

I didn't learn about any of this until I was married and on my way across the world. Everyone did their best to make the meticulously planned wedding weekend perfect for me. And for the most part, it did go off without a hitch. Unfortunately, no one could protect me from myself.

The best part of the weekend was the beginning. We had just returned from the rehearsal dinner when Pete knocked on the door to the bridal suite. "We found the pool," he said. "And it's full of... steam."

"Great," Jasmine said. "I have a sinus infection."

"We could technically skinny dip," said Pete. "You can't see a damn thing."

The whole bridal party plus significant others and assorted out-of-town friends got into bathing suits and lounged around. The pool was about half the size of a typical Olympic-sized offering, and was heated to the temperature of a hot tub. Around eleven o'clock, Nora pulled me aside. "Come into the library a second. I have something to tell you."

Someone handed me a white robe that said "Bride" on the back. Nora and I sat next to the glowing fireplace while her boyfriend Bill hovered in the background. Nora took both my hands. "Ally, Bill and I are engaged."

"Oh, Nora, that's amazing!" I said. "You guys are perfect. I'm so happy for you!"

The next morning, Sam and I discovered that our wedding suite was infiltrated with lucky ladybugs. Liz, Tina, Jasmine, Gretchen and I drove to town to get our hair and makeup done, and we spent two hours laughing and taking formal pictures around the Troutbeck grounds on a perfect spring day.

Somewhere along the way, though, I started feeling sick. I was able to take in the joy of walking down the aisle and seeing people from all areas of my life smiling at me, and I was able to look at Sam with love as I was saying my vows. But when cocktail hour started and Sam and I were in the bridal suite, having the traditional alone period called a yihud prescribed by the Jewish religion, I lost it. It was seven years later, but the situation was a perfect replica of our first college formal together. "I can't go down there!" I cried.

"Honey, you'll be fine," Sam soothed.

"No. I'm going to throw up."

"We will do this together."

Those five words from the boy turned man who was my rock motivated me to fix my dress and walk downstairs, gripping Sam's hand tightly. It was unsaid but understood that while I had been fully capable of planning a big, fancy wedding, I was not as capable of enjoying said big, fancy wedding. Since the long-ago days of high-school theater, I had grown averse to having attention squarely on me.

Getting married was also a major deal, and I was doing it without a mother like most of my friends had—a mother who was stalwartly loving, helpful, and supportive. But at the same time, I still had a mother who was the first one to sign our guest book with: "Happy wedding to my lovely daughter and wonderful son-in-law. I love you, Mommy." These contradictions threatened to bring forth emotions I simply refused to have.

It also wasn't lost on me that the "woman of steel" strategy had delivered a stable life and partner in the first place.

So I was present physically, if not mentally, for the whole affair. I walked around and greeted every table, but I barely touched the steak I'd painstakingly selected from six entrée options. I danced the hora with my bridesmaids and cut the cake with Sam, but as soon as the reception was over, I disappeared up to our room. As our friend Mike led Sam and our closest friends in a raucous piano sing-along, I was sitting alone in the dark, yanking dozens of bobby pins from my frozen hair.

When we returned from our honeymoon, Sam and I made plans to uproot our lives once again. Sam was finished with graduate school, and he, Adrienne, Pauly, and I were moving back to Chicago so Sam could do his post-doctoral fellowship at the University of Chicago. My book *Suit Yourself* was going to be published that summer, and I was leaving my job at Symbol to see if I could earn a living as a freelance writer and consultant.

In June, with Maroon 5's debut album in the CD player, our little family of four drove the fourteen hours to the Lakeview neighborhood where we'd rented an apartment sight unseen. My old boss from DDB unexpectedly offered me a part-time VP job at the office downtown, which I took in order to ensure that some money was always coming in.

I was hesitant about being back in Chicago at first, but Sam and I settled into a comfortable new lifestyle. Taking advantage of the impressive restaurant scene, we ate out several times a week and were constantly hitting concerts and street festivals.

A lot of people from Northwestern had never left the area, so we had a built-in social network. Jiao and Leo were married now and they invited us to a group gathering at a wine bar in the Streeterville neighborhood of downtown Chicago.

Sam and I were used to being New Yorkers, so we showed up wearing all black. The group had taken over a cozy corner at the front of the bar. In comparison to those in New York, Chicago establishments were huge. There could be three-hundred people in a place, and somehow no one was ever crammed together.

"Look everyone, Sam and Ally are back from the Big Apple!" Jiao said.

"Which city is better?" said Leo. "You can tell us the truth."

"I don't know yet," I said.

"Chicago has everything New York has, but it's on a more manageable scale," Sam said immediately. "It'll be better for Type As like us."

Sam and I chatted with Nora and Bill about the presidential election for a while. No matter where Sam and I went, we tended to mix with like-minded people, so political conversations in New York and Chicago were interchangeable. No one wanted to see Bush get re-elected, but Kerry seemed like a longshot.

We were introduced to some new people and reconnected with others. Then, as I came back from the bar with an amaretto sour, my ex-boyfriend Jesse appeared.

I hadn't talked to Jesse since I'd moved to New York. But unlike Ryan, who had made a pointed effort never to engage with me again, Jesse was always amenable to friendship. "Well, hey there!" I said.

We sat down to catch up. "So how's your mom doing? How's Andy?"

"I'm going to need another drink for that conversation."

I was halfway through a purposefully brief update when my cell phone beeped. "And there she is now," I said.

"Some things never change," said Jesse.

"No." The call went to voicemail, and within a minute, the phone beeped again. I put it in my purse.

Sam and I took the El back to Lakeview around midnight. The Brown Line was packed with our demographic. It was a humid summer night, and no one had anywhere to be the next morning. The neighborhood would be silent until a few hungry souls emerged for hot cinnamon rolls and mimosas at Ann Sather on Belmont.

In August, at the age of twenty-eight, I put my first book out into the world. I got a major kick out of rushing home to open the publisher's box of author copies and doing my first reading and signing at the Barnes & Noble in Lincoln Park.

The publicity for the book was scrappy but effective. After numerous online articles, a radio tour, and a few TV spots, the book started selling. Gradually, its success led to other opportunities. I was offered speaking slots at conferences, and companies wanted me to talk to their employees.

Essentially, I launched a business from nothing, and the business of Ally Golden, workplace consultant, grew so rapidly that I soon needed a concerted focus on my public brand. I hired a web designer, a social-media manager, and a public-speaking coach, because doing speeches was difficult from the start.

The plays I'd gladly participated in during high school felt a lifetime away. Now, I couldn't stand the idea of all these people looking at me. But being in front of large audiences paid better than anything else I did and also allowed me to help a lot of people at once, so I kept accepting gigs. Every time I went on stage and felt in danger of passing out, I just fought through it.

For the time being, I kept my part-time job at DDB while Sam applied to faculty positions as an assistant professor of engineering. We found out in the spring of 2005 that we'd be staying in Chicago. Sam received an offer from the Illinois Institute of Technology—around the same time Mom decided she wanted to sell her house and leave Maryland.

"Where do you want to go?" I asked late one night from my cell phone after I had already tried to hang up a few times. I sat on the front steps of our apartment building and watched a stream of disappointed Cubs fans head back downtown after an evening game.

"Providence."

"Like, Rhode Island? Why there?"

"I love the show," she replied. "It looks beautiful and quaint, and I always wanted to live in a small town."

"I think Providence is a decent-sized city, Mom. But if you think it might be good, you have to go up there and see for yourself."

Only my mother would choose a place to live based on a TV show. And while I was all in favor of a change of scenery for her, I sensed the road would be difficult. Mom barely left her house anymore. How was she going to unload it and move four hundred miles away?

"I agree," she said. "And I'm going to get a realtor in here first thing tomorrow morning. Thanks for your support, Ace."

"You're welcome," I said. "If you do the research and make a plan, I'll help you. Okay, I'm going to hang up now."

"You would come here from Chicago?"

It had started to drizzle. The Cubs fans were now moving faster under a collage of brightly colored umbrellas and bleacher cushions. I picked up my bag and headed inside. "Yes, of course."

"By the way, I finished the book. It's very engaging."

"Really?" I said, genuinely surprised. While Dad was shouting about his daughter's successful book and consulting practice from the rooftops in New York City, I didn't expect much fanfare from Mom. She wasn't much of a reader, and she didn't know anything about the corporate world. But writing was the one thing I did that she'd always cared about.

"Yes! I'm so glad I taught you to be assertive."

Sam was in front of the TV in the living room, petting Pauly and gesturing at the *Six Feet Under* opening credits. "Okay, well, I really have to go."

Mom pretended she didn't hear me and changed the subject to Al Qaeda while I tried to pay attention to the death that opened the show. Getting off the phone with her was always a delicate dance. If I got too impatient about it, she was offended. Tonight, though, I was so happy that she read my book that I didn't want to risk it. I let her chatter on as long as she wanted.

As I'd expected, the process of selling my childhood home in Gaithersburg was pretty torturous. I flew down for a weekend to meet with the realtor and clean out the house so it would be ready for showings. Sam's friend Mitch from Northwestern, who was now living in Washington, DC, graciously offered to help Tina and me. The three of us worked the whole day while Mom slept off a migraine.

I thought of all my friends who still slept in relatively untouched childhood bedrooms when they came home. As with other things, this was far from my experience. I'd ceased to have my own room in the house when I was still in college. And I didn't have many personal things left there period, since over the years, Mom and Andy had made a big show out of getting rid of something important to me every time my behavior displeased them. I shipped just two boxes, mostly of mementos and photo albums, back to Chicago.

As I was getting ready to fly home, I noticed our fourteen-year-old cat, Magic, dragging her back legs as she tried to walk. "Mom, has Magic done this before?"

Mom looked shocked. "No, never. It looks like she had a stroke."

I postponed my flight so we could take the cat to the vet. Mom and I sat in the waiting room together, silent tears rolling down our cheeks. Mom was right about the stroke, and the doctor wasn't sure Magic would be able to walk again. The question of whether we'd have to put her to sleep hung in the air as I hugged Mom and assured her we'd do everything we could before we gave up.

A week later, Magic was worse, and Mom took her back to the vet to end her suffering. "And I had to do it by myself," she said bitterly. "You're never here when I need you."

Caught up in my own grief, I could only agree with her. "I wish I had been there. I should have been there. We just didn't know what was going to happen."

After Magic's death, Mom slid a little further downhill, and progress toward selling the house stalled. She had to make a series of expensive improvements that the twenty-five-year-old house needed and some that it shouldn't have needed (like getting my brother's basement-finishing project up to code). She had the house staged but then couldn't keep it clean and free of clutter.

But the biggest holdup was this: the realtor could not get Mom to leave the house during showings. Whether he gave her a lot of notice or no notice, whether the appointments were at seven in the morning or seven at night, Mom was inevitably asleep in her bed when people showed up.

We were finally able to sell the house, sight unseen, to a buyer who wanted to flip it. I was sentimental. For better and worse, this was the place where I grew up, and soon it would be no more. Mom now had to be out in a month. She'd never visited Providence as she'd promised but now wanted to drive up there with three cats, no apartment, and no job. And I was going to help her do it.

The lucky thing about Providence in particular was that there was a clinic at Butler Hospital, affiliated with Brown University. It specialized in the treatment of what I was now sure was my mother's primary diagnosis, borderline personality disorder (BPD). Butler's dialectical behavior program was advertised as helping women who "live chaotic, painful, lives," "have fears of being abandoned," "have trouble staying sober," and "feel suicidal much of the time."

Check, check, check.

Most people understand the concept of depression, but personality disorders are a little tougher. We all have personalities that impact the way we perceive ourselves, other people, and our environment. When someone has a personality disorder, personality traits become so inflexible that they negatively impact the ability to have healthy relationships, to function normally in the world.

The various personality disorders, including BPD, are described in the *DSM-V* (*Diagnostic and Statistical Manual of Mental Disorders*). They frequently overlap. Because people with these disorders see their interactions in a skewed light, they can never get what they need from other people. And the more they manipulate, the more others turn away. Naturally, this cycle often results in severe depression.

Through a connection of Sam's, I was able to score an appointment for my mother to be evaluated by the director of the Butler clinic, and I flew to Maryland to get her up there in time for it. I spent a majority of my first twenty-four hours in town packing for the movers we'd hired. As soon as I was done, I loaded Mom and the three cat carriers into her silver Infinity, and we set out for New England. We drove out of the neighborhood, the town, and the state that had been Mom's home for thirty years without ceremony. The cats meowed pitifully for most of the five-hour drive. I knew how they felt.

When we arrived in Providence, it was dark and difficult to see. We checked into a pet-friendly budget hotel and tried to sleep so we'd be ready to go apartment hunting in the morning. At seven o'clock, I was ready to go. Mom, however, was not.

"I have a headache," she said.

"Mom, the movers are coming in two days, and we don't have an address to send them to," I replied. "We have to go."

"I never should have done this."

I resisted the urge to agree with her. "You weren't making any progress in Gaithersburg," I pointed out instead. "Your evaluation with Butler Hospital is tomorrow. But we need to find you a place to live."

We looked at each other. Mom's hair was gathered into a ponytail with the end sticking straight up on her head, like a stalk. I handed her a brush, and she reluctantly followed me outside to the car. I drove her around Providence, mostly in circles due to the city's strange traffic patterns. It was immediately apparent that this was not the quaint little town Mom had loved from NBC. Much of Providence looked a little worse for wear, with lots of buildings showing their two-hundred-year age.

"It's so ugly," Mom complained. It made sense that she would feel this way, since she had spent decades living in fairly pristine communities.

"You wanted old. I bet the beach is lovely in the summer."

"I wanted to live *on* the beach."

"Then you're not living in Providence; you're living in Newport," I said, my irritation starting to show.

Fortunately, the downtown area was reasonable. We identified a new-construction apartment building with one- and two-bedroom units that was next to a supermarket and a mall. Butler Hospital was a five-minute drive, and best of all, they had a vacancy for Mom to move in right away.

We drove back to the hotel to feed the cats and await the movers. The next morning, I almost had to physically drag Mom to the car so we could drive to Butler. She wore a faded T-shirt and trench coat over a pair of ancient navy khakis. I recalled the Mom of my youth, who never left the house without a fully color-coordinated clothing, shoe, and accessory ensemble and always had to have flawless hair, makeup, and nails. The woman in front of me now was only sixty, but I was starting to think that assisted living might have been a better option. Well, at least Dr. Patrick would know exactly what he was dealing with.

The doctor talked with Mom and me together, and then with Mom and me separately. He asked Mom tons of questions about her physical- and mental-health history and took rapid notes. I waited desperately for him to tell me that Mom could have a spot in his outpatient dialectical behavior program. But at the end of the evaluation, he clasped his hands together and looked at us gravely.

"This program will help you," he said to my mother. "But you aren't ready for it yet."

"I don't need it," my mother said, as if that was the message she heard.

"You need it, but our form of therapy won't do you any good unless you get off all these medications you're on. We can't treat Susan, because we can't even know Susan at the moment."

"I need every one of these drugs," Mom insisted. "They are all for physical issues. If I weren't constantly so ill, I would function fine."

Mom required drugs to wake up in the morning, drugs to leave the house during the day, and drugs to go to sleep at night. Many were narcotics. Her prescription history was so complicated I'd lost track of the medications she'd stopped using and those that were her current go-tos.

Dr. Patrick had apparently heard this story before and wasn't buying the pain-management argument. "I can recommend a detox program here in Providence."

"Can I just come and talk to you first?" Mom said.

"I'm afraid it doesn't work that way. Tell me, Susan, are you motivated to make some changes?"

"I've been dancing as fast as I can for sixty years. I don't know why, but God has been punishing me for sixty years. I'm too tired for change. If you had my life, you'd be tired too."

She was perfectly sane when she said it too. No psychiatric hospital was going to involuntarily admit my mother for an attitude like that, and no outpatient program could force her to take responsibility for her own well-being.

We had no choice but to leave. But on our way out, the doctor handed me a copy of a book called *Stop Walking on Eggshells* and advised me to see my own therapist in Chicago. That night, our last in the hotel, I thumbed through the book. Much of it confirmed what I had already researched online, which was that people with borderline personality disorder have a pattern of unstable relationships, switching quickly from idealizing other people to devaluing them and feeling like others don't care or give enough. "Because people with BPD have a hard time integrating a person's good and bad traits, their current opinion of someone is often based on their last interaction with them—like someone who lacks a short-term memory," said the authors.

Interesting observation.

The book discussed the sudden and dramatic changes in self-image, characterized by shifting goals, values, and vocational aspirations. I thought of all my mother's grand career plans, none of which had materialized. And I liked the line from DBT pioneer Marsha Linehan, who said: "People with BPD are like people with third degree burns over 90 percent of their body. Lacking emotional skin, they feel agony at the slightest touch or movement." Indeed, my mother was a classic case of a BPD who tried to ease her desperation by self-medicating with drugs.

There was a whole section about the hell that children of BPD parents go through. I took a pen out of my purse and highlighted the recommended coping strategies, including seeking support and validation via online and offline support groups, setting and sticking to boundaries, and detaching with love. Watching my mother sleep, her mouth slightly open, covers pulled up to her chin, I considered how unsuccessful I'd been at doing any of these things.

When the movers from Maryland showed up the next morning, Mom, the cats, and I were waiting for them in her new and empty one-bedroom apartment. While they were unloading, I went to the supermarket to get some food for the fridge. We spent the rest of the day setting up as best we could, though at least twenty boxes were still piled in the living room. Mom had gotten excited about meeting some Jewish men in the area, so I set up a Match.com profile for her, and she dressed up so I could take a few photos.

Before I flew back to Chicago, I worked with the building's management to hire a service in which a woman named Jill would come to Mom's apartment and help her get organized and locate resources. I didn't have much hope for the Butler program since Mom wasn't motivated to detox, but I hoped she could at least find a good psychiatrist in Providence.

She'd wanted a new life, the chance to start over, but predictably, she wasn't happy. "I can't believe you're just going to leave me here," she said.

Guilt. Again. "Mom, what am I supposed to do?"

"You could have stayed at least a week."

"I have a job." Except my job was flexible, and I didn't have to travel to any speaking engagements in the next few weeks. I was going home because the five days I'd already spent with Mom was too much for me. And we both knew it.

"I'm alone here."

I put my arm around her. "I know. But you were alone in Gaithersburg too. You can do anything you want here. Jill's going to help you, and I'll come back to visit in a couple of months."

"That Butler program's not for me, you know. And to think we built it up so much."

"Nothing's going to be an easy fix at this point, Mom. You really have to want to get better."

"I don't have the money to pay for it anyway."

"If there was anything worth spending your money on..."

"Easy for you to say. You're not the one who's going to starve."

I could have kept going. Rationalizing was, after all, my forte. But I saw a million excuses in her eyes and didn't feel like waiting around for the one in which I was to blame. Mom didn't hate me at this moment, so I should quit while I was ahead. I kissed her on the cheek and left.

Sam and I bought a house in Elmhurst, a semi-liberal, urban/suburban enclave west of downtown Chicago. We found it after another house we'd bid on failed inspection due to an illegal hair salon in the basement. The home, on a quiet, tree-lined block next to a Catholic church, was a bungalow with white siding and green shutters and trim. I loved every minute of poring through catalogues from

Restoration Hardware and West Elm and choosing paint colors, furniture, and decor.

Once we were fully moved in, I returned to Providence to check on Mom. She'd befriended Jill, the woman whom we'd hired to help her run errands and find her way around the new city. I took them both out for an expensive tapas dinner and to the movies, but my attempt at a normal evening couldn't disguise the fact that my mother still skated on the edge of total dysfunction. She seemed no happier in Providence than she had in Gaithersburg, except now we were paying a fortune in rent, and Mom was far away from all of her doctors.

Regretting the role I'd played in the move, I bought Mom a ticket to come see our new house. I hoped the effort it would take to pack and get herself to the airport would spur her to action in other areas of her life.

She did come, and once she even got up early enough to sit at my kitchen table with a cup of chamomile tea while I made breakfast and cleaned a new set of All-Clad pots Sam and I had received for our wedding. I'd hung light blue curtains in the large bay window, and splashes of cool morning sunshine hit our faces.

"Can I use Brillo on these?" I asked my mother.

She considered the question. "I think you better not. You haven't even used them. How dirty can they be?"

'It feels so good to finally have a place to put all this stuff. You want some eggs?"

"Thanks."

I examined my fingers. "I need to do something about my hands. It's the middle of the summer and they're still all cracked."

"How often do you wash them? I have some cream you can try. And come to think of it, you should also use it on your elbows."

"My elbows?"

"I've aged there very quickly."

"What do you mean? Like wrinkles?"

It was the most mundane scene you could imagine. I took a mental picture and vowed to store it at the front of my memory forever.

"Yes. It's from all the dryness," Mom said. "I keep hearing planes. There must be an airport nearby."

"There isn't," I insisted.

"You never believe anything I say. Look it up. Dollars to doughnuts I'm right."

Admittedly, I usually didn't put too much stock in her commentary. I understood that it was insulting, but I viewed it as her fault for using up all her credibility. When I flipped open my laptop to investigate, I grudgingly nodded. "You're partially right. There's no airport here, but Elmhurst is often in flight paths bound for O'Hare."

"See?" she said triumphantly. "I told you I wasn't hearing things."

It was a good visit, and when Mom went back to Providence, she called me every day. Given that I had two jobs, was working on a second book, and traveled often for speeches that drained me physically and mentally, I didn't always have the energy to talk to her. This did not go over well, and in the early winter of 2006, my mother decided to do something about it.

"What do you mean, she disappeared?" my brother said irritably.

"I mean, I've been calling her for a week. I always get her voice mail, and she doesn't call me back."

"Come on, Ally, she's done this before."

"No, she hasn't!" I cried. "And how would you know anyway? You haven't talked to her in five years."

"Something like that," he mused. "Look, why don't you call the building manager? They can go upstairs and check on her."

This had occurred to me, of course, but I was terrified about what it meant. That it was actually an emergency. That Mom hadn't called me back because she was dead.

In the end, I did it anyway. The building manager knocked on the door of my mother's apartment, and she answered immediately. When the manager mentioned that I was very worried, Mom acted like she didn't know what he was talking about.

Only to me would she later admit that she had sat next to her answering machine day after day, listening to me record increasingly desperate messages. "Now you know how I feel when you ignore me," she said calmly.

Caught in a valley between rage and relief, I said: "Just don't do that again, all right?" As if I had any control over whether she did or not.

Mom's next vehicle to get my attention was an announcement that she planned to move back to Maryland after less than a year in Providence. She demanded that I fly out and help her. When I refused, insisting that she give her life there a chance—starting with Butler's detox program—she was furious.

"As usual, everything you have to do is more important than me," she hissed. "I'll be gone soon, and you'll regret not having a mother every day of your life."

I begged my therapist and the online community at BPDFamily to tell me I was doing the right thing. It didn't really matter what anyone said, though. I was constantly tortured by thoughts of what might happen to my mother.

It turned out that my concerns were well founded. That was a problem I'd had for a long time. People with anxiety often worry about things that never come to pass. But usually, when I freaked out, it was for a good reason. When I freaked out that something bad would happen, it often did.

Solid information about my mother's situation during her last week in Providence came to me in bits and pieces. I will probably never have the full story. I learned that Mom had experienced some sort of overdose, had called for help, and had been hospitalized. I learned that she had had all three of her cats put to sleep, though it wasn't clear if this occurred before or after the overdose. And I learned that after being discharged, she had called movers and an apartment complex in Gaithersburg and had driven herself back to Maryland.

"Why did you do it?" I whispered.

I wasn't sure exactly what I meant by this. Why did she overdose? Why did she put her cats down? Why did she move?

"I wanted to go home. I had no help, and I wanted to move. I couldn't put the cats through that again. It would have been too cruel."

No, Mom, I thought. Cruel is killing three innocent and perfectly healthy animals because you didn't feel like dealing with them anymore. As I considered the fact that she'd always favored her pets over her human children, I had to wonder: what might have happened if she'd been this sick when Andy and I were younger?

My mother's situation at this point had become difficult to fathom and even more difficult to explain. I stopped talking to everyone about it, but every week I actually became more entrenched. Mom might have been back in Gaithersburg, but there was no one left from her former life. Speaking with her long-time longtime financial advisor, I learned that the money situation was now dire. A little over ten years earlier, Mom could have been set for life. Now, she had less than $25,000 and no income coming in.

Sam insisted that we would not support her financially if she continued to refuse treatment. But I couldn't allow her to end up on the street, either. Late that summer, I flew to Maryland to tap every community-based resource I could get my hands on. Through the Montgomery County Department of Social Services, I secured a caseworker who would connect her with health care and help get her affairs in order. We also applied for early Social Security so Mom could begin getting a monthly check. I was so busy driving around hither and yon that I scarcely had time to notice that Mom looked like the ordeal in Providence had aged her ten years, weighing less than ninety pounds, with the haggard appearance of a cancer patient.

I had no choice but to face it when Mom took me back to her new apartment after we'd had shrimp platters, salad, and cheddar biscuits at her favorite restaurant, Red Lobster. It was only partially unpacked after a couple of months, and on the bare white wall above her bed was a DNR (do not resuscitate) sign handwritten in stark black marker. She had a photo album of my grandmother's, and as we paged through it carefully, Mom shared the stories she knew of her family's history in the old country. When we came upon a person I didn't recognize, Mom turned the faded photo over and wrote the name in neat, black script.

I had the distinct feeling that this would be the last time I'd see her.

We sat on her bed together for a long time, both of us recognizing at least on some level that the ship was sinking. I turned her hand over in mine—the skin looked translucent, and her rings slid up and down her fingers. I gave her all the affection she could never get enough of; I told her I loved her and that I hated seeing her in pain. I tried to assure her that we would get back on the right track, but the words were hollow for both of us. And then I drove away in my yellow rental coupe, watching her stand on her balcony and wave.

That fall, Sam and I decided to have a baby. The decision was not made lightly. I was deeply troubled by the possibility that through my genes, I could pass on the mental illness that ran rampant through my family. Over time, however, Sam convinced me that even if the child had a predisposition to depression or anxiety, we could catch it early and initiate proper treatment. Through good parenting, he said, we could "mold" certain traits out of the kid. And besides, if we chose to adopt, we had no idea what we were going to get. What if a child from another family had a more problematic genetic load than I did?

In the end, the desire to create the close and loving immediate family I'd never known wore me down. Plus, now Sam and I wouldn't feel that we had to rent a kid every time we went out in procreation-central Elmhurst. Sam and I proceeded with testing to rule out the more common Jewish genetic disorders, and when we were given the all clear, we started trying. I was thirty years old, and getting pregnant didn't take especially long. After only a few months, I was suddenly throwing up everything I ate and walking a mile to get Popeyes fried chicken and biscuits at seven in the morning. When it finally occurred to me to buy a test, I was already six weeks along. The baby was due in September 2007.

Sam and I were ecstatic, but our enthusiasm waned when my pregnancy induced a panicked state in my mother. This entity that didn't even weigh a pound yet had already rendered her a second-class citizen, and Mom stepped up her efforts to keep me tethered. One frigid January afternoon, I was walking home from the train I took to my DDB job in the city, and from a block away, I saw that something major had happened on my lawn. As I got closer, I saw several piles of cardboard moving boxes. They were all addressed to me and postmarked Gaithersburg. In the first one I ripped open, I saw my mother's fine china wrapped in newspaper.

I dialed Mom's cell phone before I even went into the house. "Mom, what am I supposed to do with all this stuff?"

"It's yours now," she said simply. "I won't be here much longer."

"Come on, Mom," I begged. "Don't do this. You're going to be a grandma soon."

"That's true," she said. "And once you have that baby, I won't mean anything to you."

Sam and I took the boxes inside and put them in the basement. There was nothing else to do. And I called my mother every day to make sure she was still alive, my heart beating faster every time the phone rang repeatedly or her voice mail clicked on. Then, one Sunday in February, Sam and I were driving to a friend's baby shower in Chicago and were sideswiped by a car darting into traffic from an alley. The Saturn was totaled, and because I was pregnant, the paramedics who arrived on the scene wanted to make sure I wasn't injured. Even though I felt fine, I consented to being taken to the hospital for an ultrasound.

The ER resident scanned my belly for what seemed like a very long time. "How far along did you say you were?"

"I'll be twelve weeks tomorrow," I replied. "Hooray for the end of the first trimester!" She refused to smile or say anything else. "Is the baby okay?" I asked anxiously.

Finally, she said quietly: "I'm going to send the attending doctor in, okay?"

They didn't make us wait. Not even a few minutes. The attending sat down next to Sam and me. "We're still waiting for the results of your blood work to come back," she said. "But you are certain that you are twelve weeks?"

"Positive," I said. "We heard the baby's heartbeat at eight weeks, and that was a month ago."

She paused. "I'm so sorry, Allison. But it looks like your little one probably stopped developing shortly after the eight-week mark. It's far too small for twelve weeks, and there is no heartbeat."

"The baby is dead?" Sam said.

"I'm afraid so. This is often nature's response when something goes wrong during the fetus's development. Allison's body is likely preparing to miscarry."

"But this has nothing to do with the accident?" I asked.

"No."

I just stared at her, my stomach clamping like a vise. "What do I do?"

"After we confirm the situation with the blood work, there will be two options," she said gently. "You can wait to begin bleeding naturally, or we can do a D and C. It's a minor operation to remove the remaining fetal tissue from the uterus."

I struggled to keep my voice even. "I want the operation. I want it out."

Sam and I took a taxi home, stunned. When you're pregnant for the first time and got that way fairly easily, it never occurs to you that something can go wrong. We later found out that up to 25 percent of all conceptions end in miscarriage, but that didn't stop us from feeling like hell as I was rolled into the operating room to have the remains of our first baby scraped out.

As soon as I got home, I called Mom. As always, she loved hearing from me when something awful had happened. And as always, she knew the right thing to say. The women in our family were very fertile, she claimed. This baby wasn't meant to be, but another one would come soon, and she couldn't wait to come and help me at the birth. That wouldn't happen, of course, but I appreciated the sentiment. The next call I placed was to my OB/GYN. Jesse and I had been talking about going snowboarding in Wisconsin, and I wanted to see when that would be safe. After my doctor said I could basically do whatever I wanted, we made plans to go the next day.

It had only been a week since the car accident, and though Sam had been driving at the time, I found myself hesitant to get behind the wheel. The highway north from Chicago was empty, so Jesse let me practice in his car. Now that I was married and Jesse always had some girlfriend or another, we'd settled into an easy friendship. I put an old Duncan Sheik album into the CD player, and Jesse fell asleep against the passenger-side window, while I drove and dispassionately observed that I should probably be at home crying over my medically induced miscarriage instead of playing hooky from work in the mountains. But although I had no medication left in my body, I once again had the sensation of existing outside my body and mind. Except for some hard-core soreness from all the times I fell on the ice, I felt absolutely nothing.

Life went on. My father was diagnosed with prostate cancer and needed to have surgery to remove it, so I flew to New York to help him. And as my doctor mandated, Sam and I waited a couple of months to try for another baby. Then, we were at his cousin's wedding and the filet mignon sent me running to the bathroom with my hand over my mouth. At first I thought my wedding aversion was back, but then it occurred to me that I was probably pregnant again. Sam and I bought a test on the way home, and it was positive.

This time around, I was highly vigilant about my condition. I was throwing up so much that I couldn't go to work, so my doctor thankfully prescribed an antiemetic. When I told Mom I was expecting again, she sounded almost disappointed. "I have some news too," she said.

I hoped her announcement had something to do with the fact that she'd finally received her first Social Security check, but I doubted it. "What?" I said warily.

"I bought a gun."

"You what?"

"I have a gun."

"What in the hell do you need a gun for?"

"You know the reason. A gun is foolproof."

My heart rate jumped up its typical twenty beats at this latest bombshell. "How did you even get it?"

"I have resources."

Perversely, I was proud of her. She couldn't seem to do anything to help herself, but somehow she'd pulled this off. "Mom, please tell me you're not going to play around with it."

"I'm not going to do anything with it—for now."

Later that week, I told my therapist that I didn't want to be afraid all the time, that with this new baby growing inside me, I couldn't be. It wasn't fair to him or her. I'd neglected my own emotional well-being my whole life, but my health wasn't mine to discard anymore. God forbid I have another miscarriage. My first priority from now on had to be to take care of this little one.

My therapist gently suggested that it was time to sever contact with Mom. "You can give her some conditions," she said. "Tell her that you will communicate with her by letter or e-mail, but that you won't speak to her until she can prove to you that she is taking steps to get the help she needs."

"I've never gone that far," I said uncertainly. "If I step back from her now, who knows what will happen?"

The doctor nodded. "That's what you need to think about. You've done a remarkable job of keeping your mother here for years. But she needs to live for herself, and when you drop the rope, you need to be prepared for the worst. She may finally go through with it, and that would not be your fault."

I wondered where she'd gotten the phrase "drop the rope." A parable she shared at the end of the visit provided the answer.

"The Bridge"

There was a man who had given much thought to what he wanted from life. He had experienced many moods and trials. He had experimented with different ways of living, and he had had his share of both success and failure. At last, he had begun to see clearly where he wanted to go. Eager to arrive, he started on his journey. With each step, he wanted to move faster; with each thought about his goal, his heart beat quicker; with each vision of what lay ahead, he found renewed vigor.

Hurrying along, he came upon a bridge that crossed through the middle of a town. It had been built high above a river in order to protect it from the floods of spring. He started across. Then he noticed someone coming from the opposite direction. When they were within hailing distance, he could see that the other had a rope around his waist. The other began to uncurl the rope, and, just as they were coming close, the stranger said, "Pardon me, would you be so kind as to hold the end a moment?"

Surprised by this politely phrased but curious request, he agreed without a thought, reached out, and took it. "Thank you," said the other. "Two hands now, and remember, hold tight." Then, the other jumped off the bridge. Quickly, the free-falling body hurtled the distance of the rope's length, and from the bridge, the man abruptly felt the pull. Instinctively, he held tight and was almost dragged over the side.

"Why did you do this?" the man called out.

"I am your responsibility now," said the other. "If you let go, I will be lost."

"But I cannot pull you up," the man cried. He began to look around for help, but there was no one. Fearing that his arms could not hold out much longer, he tied the rope around his waist. What should he do? If he let go, all his life he would know that he let this other die. If he stayed, he risked losing momentum toward his own long-sought-after salvation. With ironic humor, he thought to die himself, instantly, to jump off the bridge while he was still holding on. But he wanted to live and live fully.

A new thought occurred to him. While he could not pull this other up solely by his own efforts, if the other would shorten the rope from his end by curling it around his waist again and again, together, they could do it! "Now listen," he shouted down. "I think I know how to save you." And he explained his plan. But the other wasn't interested. "You mean you won't help? But I told you I cannot pull you up myself, and I don't think I can hang on much longer either."

"You must try," the other shouted back in tears. "If you fail, I die!"

"I want you to listen carefully," the man said. "I will not accept the position of choice for your life, only for my own; the position of choice for your own life I give back to you."

"You cannot mean what you say!" the other yelled. "What could be so important that you would let someone die?"

The man waited a moment. There was no change in the tension of the rope. "I accept your choice," he said, at last, and freed his hands.

—Edwin H. Friedman

I printed out a copy of the parable and kept it on my desk as I wrestled with the guilt of walking away from my mother after a lifetime of actively trying to save her.

"She gave in way too easily," I told Sam. "She said I was always cutting her off, and she didn't see how this time was any different."

"It's different because this time you mean it," he replied.

"Do I? I don't know."

"Yes you do. We've gone on like this way too long."

I noted his use of the word "we." And it was true. I had dragged Sam on the odyssey with Mom for almost ten years. Every time she said something to hurt me or did something to manipulate me, Sam had to listen and react. I might have been exhausted, but he was tired too.

But still. I thought about Mom every day and fought violently against the urge to call her and pretend like the ultimatum had never happened. I sent her a Mother's Day card accompanied by a long letter and my ultrasound picture. I received a short, formal letter in return. Its reserved tone nearly ripped me in half. My mother had given up on me.

I mailed a birthday card in early fall. No response this time. I ached for reassurance, but no matter how many people told me I was well within my rights, that I was doing what was best for the baby, it wasn't enough. I had released the rope, but having to stand on the bridge and watch what happened felt like a greater punishment than anything my mother could inflict.

On Saturday afternoon, November 3, 2007, I was sitting on the floor, wrapping a birthday present for a friend, when our doorbell rang. An Elmhurst police officer stood on the steps. "I need to speak to Allison Golden, please."

"That's me," I said.

"Ma'am, I've had a call from a unit in Montgomery County, Maryland. There has been an incident."

I froze. "What happened?"

"I'm afraid I can't share specifics, but the detective there would like for you to call him right away."

Sam had joined me at the door. "A detective?" he said, shaking his head as if trying to clear it.

I took out my cell phone. "What's the number?"

It took Sam and me a few hours to reach the detective live. The Elmhurst police officer did not confirm or deny that a death was involved, but something about the way this was playing out was different from previous situations with either Mom or Andy.

At around seven that evening, I learned that my mother had killed herself.

The circumstances shocked even me, who had been anticipating this outcome my whole life. Early that morning, Mom had walked into the woods behind her apartment complex, put a .38-caliber revolver in her mouth, and pulled the trigger. A neighbor found the body next to a jogging path a few hours later.

I was given a lot of information—most of it passing through like ambient noise. The detective was closing the investigation, as Mom's death had been ruled a suicide rather than a homicide. The body was with the coroner, and I needed to make arrangements for it. Mom had left her will and a cassette tape on her kitchen counter labeled with my name.

When I put down the phone, it was as if, for years, I had been standing motionless in a frozen world, the snow silent, glistening icicles suspended from trees. The day my mother died, the wind roared, the snow kicked up a furious dance, and the icicles crashed to the ground. I sank to my knees, Sam holding on to me as if he could somehow stop the crushing grief from burying me.

That first night, I couldn't stop shaking. I felt this overwhelming fear of nothing in particular. I'd worried about this event for as long as I could remember, and once it happened, it seemed as if some sort of visceral response had been set off. I couldn't stand to be alone at all for three days, and while I had no trouble falling asleep at night, I would inevitably wake up a few hours later and stay that way, my mother's last moments in the woods branded on my brain.

I wanted to be open about my feelings so that my now-traditional manner of repression wouldn't hurt the baby. But every time I cried, I didn't like it. Despite being the appropriate response, the loss of control was unnerving. And even though the few friends I chose to tell were wonderfully supportive—about a dozen people came over for the Jewish mourning ritual of Shiva, Nora met me for dinner all the time, and Jesse just let me lie on his living-room couch and stare at the ceiling—I felt alienated and only able to talk about what had happened in an intellectual, detached manner.

My mother was cremated. She'd asked for her ashes to be scattered on the beach, which had always been her favorite place. I wanted to wait awhile, though. We didn't have a funeral. There wasn't much of a point. I wouldn't be able to stand in the center of buffeting well-wishers, with this person sharing a funny story about Mom and that person hugging me tightly and assuring me that my mother had made a difference in so many lives. No one loved her but me, so I grieved alone.

I'd never been much of a spooner, preferring instead to curl up in my corner of our king-sized bed. But after my mother died, I fell asleep clinging to Sam and often stayed attached to him for half the night. While working at home, I crept around the house carefully, as if expecting to see my mother's ghost around every corner.

I took the train into Chicago to see my therapist, the same one who'd accurately predicted the timeline of Mom's death. In a week, all the leaves had disappeared from the trees. The naked branches shook in the brisk air.

"Oh, Ally, I'm so sorry," she said. "How are you doing?"

"I keep thinking about her life. It was more tragic than her death."

She nodded. "She went through a lot. You too."

"The last thirteen years especially." I paused. "I can't stop thinking about it."

"What happened in the woods, you mean?"

"I mean, this was inevitable, right?" I said. "And in more than one way, it was the best outcome. She's out of pain. But it was just…so gruesome, so violent. I never thought for one second it would happen this way."

"She still managed to surprise you."

"You know what the worst thing is? She was so resourceful about it, so precise. She got it done. I keep thinking, what if she had applied a fraction of these abilities to her life? Things might have been different."

"Yes."

"And the courage. Jesus. Can you imagine how hard it must have been to pull the…"

I trailed off, tears pooling. I had been sitting Indian style on her couch, my usual position when I wanted to be comfortable. But I felt myself straightening up, crossing one knee over the other as one does in a business meeting.

"Ally, my heart is just breaking for you."

I watched her face. She looked like she was about to start crying herself. Instantly, my tears were sucked back into their ducts. I didn't want to talk anymore. I just wanted to go home.

Sam and I lied about the specifics of Mom's death to most of the people we told, including nonclose friends, coworkers, and our bosses. I assumed that was the right thing to do with suicide, since it carried a stigma after all. Although the lying was incredibly stressful—I was so discombobulated I couldn't remember who knew what—the sense of shame associated with the truth was worse. Somehow, I couldn't help feeling like my mother's action reflected on me.

Exactly one week after my mother went into the woods, I dreamed that she was standing in front of me in her pajamas. She told me right away that she was dead, and as I tried to hug her, my arms passed right through her body. I said that I hoped she was happier now and at peace, and she replied that she wasn't. The physical pain was gone, she shared, but she was very concerned that my brother would get his hands on any remaining money. It was as if her sole goal in appearing was to prevent that from happening.

Despite Mom's "warning," I did allow Andy to clean out her apartment instead of going down there myself. Sam thought being among my mother's things would send me over the edge. My friend Tina, who still lived in Maryland, graciously agreed to accompany Andy to make sure I'd be able to have any items that might be important to me. I wasn't sure I believed my brother's claim that there were no prescription drugs in the apartment, and concluding that it no longer mattered what Mom was or wasn't on felt strange.

Sam connected me with the American Foundation for Suicide Prevention, which was doing a webcast panel for survivors. I called in, but paradoxically, I felt even more isolated after listening. Everyone talked about how they were completely shocked by their relatives' acts. No one spoke of the "will she or won't she?" experience that had categorized my life for twenty years. It also bothered me when the speakers discussed the long process of recovery. I was about to have a baby, and I wanted this to be over. And now, I had this fear of spontaneously combusting six months from now. And the number of panelists with multiple suicides in the same immediate family—for God's sake. I worried about Andy and felt a fresh surge of doubt about conceiving the baby kicking inside me right at that moment.

November slid into December. Every day was different. Sometimes I felt normal, sometimes not quite right, and other times devastated. On the days when it seemed like nothing had happened, I was guilty. This was objectively one of the worst things that could happen to anyone. What did it say about me that I could function this well?

As the event of her death got further away, I started to grieve Mom's life. I put a picture of her at age thirty on the mantel in our living room, wishing I could know her again as that seemingly happy, loving, and productive woman. This was a mother I could actually miss, unlike the person she'd been over the last decade. This was a mother I could mourn, unlike the person who didn't have enough relationships to warrant a funeral, who hadn't contributed anything to society in years, and who couldn't even look forward to having a grandchild.

Thinking about the totality of her suffering over a sixty-three-year-long lifetime, I was no longer convinced I could blame her for anything she'd done to me. On the one hand, she was clearly ill, unable to see and cope with reality. But on the other, she often didn't follow the path to help that others painstakingly laid out for her. Did Mom do the best she could, or not? I didn't know the answer.

On the last day of 2007, I went downstairs in a plush blue bathrobe. The baby was getting so big that the garment barely fit. Sam was making blueberry pancakes and I sat at the table, watching him.

"I want to listen to the tape," I said suddenly.

Sam turned off the stove and looked at me. "Really? Are you sure?"

Mom's tape, which had essentially functioned as her suicide note, had been on the top shelf of the hall closet since the Montgomery County police had mailed it to me. "Yeah," I said. "Tomorrow's a new year."

"Do you want to eat first?"

I shook my head.

Sam retrieved the tape and put it in the old stereo that was rarely used for anything. "Do you want me to hear it?"

"No," I said. "It's supposed to be for me."

He put the pancakes on a plate and went upstairs.

A few years back, Sam and I had gone to Costa Rica with Liz and John. We went zip-lining in the jungle, and the first part required jumping off a high platform into nothingness. This felt similar, with fear seizing hold of my imagination. Whatever was on this tape, I would not be able to un-hear it.

My mother came through the speakers. It was a voice I'd heard since I was in utero. A voice I'd heard more days than not. A voice I hadn't heard in six months. A voice I would never hear again in this life.

The baby kicked and rolled gently inside me. Pauly came over and nuzzled his face against my bare legs. I chewed on a stray piece of hair as my mother talked, sounding desperately sad, desperately lonely. I closed my eyes against the pain. No human being should have to feel like this, but especially not the one who had once given me everything.

Mom acknowledged her role in the course her life had taken, but she stopped short of genuine accountability. "From childhood, I never got the handbook on how to have a happy life," she said. "And I've never been able to do anything about that."

She didn't seem to harbor a grudge that I'd cut off phone contact, but her attribution was a simple "You never liked me."

She still could not see how much I had suffered, how awful it had been to set boundaries with her during the time when I needed a mother most. She told me that she loved me, and that she knew I loved her, and that she was sorry she wouldn't meet her grandchild.

At the end of the tape was a great gift, perhaps the most important one my mother had given me in thirty years. "I did think about hearing your voice one last time, but I've decided not to call," she said. "You can't do anything to help me and knowing my plan will only cause you stress."

In this one instance, my mother actually thought about how her actions would affect me. It was this gift that allowed me to shut off the tape—and walk into my future—with the knowledge that on some level, my mother could love me.

Sam and I were having a baby boy, and most of early 2008 was consumed preparing for his March birth. I read a lot of baby books, slowly establishing my identity as a "mother." The timing was ideal, for I'd keenly felt the loss of my identity as "tortured adult child of a mentally ill mother."

I read aloud to Sam from the website BabyCenter.com. I was part of a March 2008 birth club with a thousand members. We exchanged information about everything from Braxton Hicks contractions to BPA-free bottles. "Baby boys tend to pee as soon as the diaper is removed, so when changing them, do not allow the old diaper to fall open. Keeping the diaper up forms a shield between you and the baby, preventing the pee from striking you in the face."

"There's a whole article about that?" Sam said.

"Oh no. There are twenty articles about that."

"Come on. What's so bad about getting peed on?"

"I'm telling you right now that puking is your department. That's where I draw the line."

If there was a piece of advice about child-rearing, I wanted to hear it, no matter how scary or disheartening. I had more available mental energy than ever before, and as the baby's existence became more concrete, he took over more and more of it.

Starting in December, I had a parade of baby showers in Chicago and New York. By the time my department at DDB threw the last one on Friday, February 29, I'd become a pro at opening pastel-wrapped packages and cooing over the contents.

It was a good thing Sam and I had put everything away in the baby's nursery and set up his crib ahead of time, because the day after my work shower, I felt very odd. I wasn't due for another four weeks, so I attributed it to having a cold with a low-grade fever. On Saturday night, though, I woke up at four thirty soaking wet. I thought maybe the baby's weight had collapsed my bladder, since that had happened before. But when I explained my symptoms to the doctor on call, she was convinced my water had broken. Sam and I had better go to the hospital.

The contractions ramped up quickly, but nevertheless, I was able to walk myself into the Prentice Woman's Hospital in downtown Chicago and casually tell the triage nurse that I was in labor. I was in the hospital for a total of ten minutes before a resident examined me and said, alarmed: "I am holding your baby's foot, Ms. Golden, and we need to do an emergency cesarian. Things are going to move very quickly, but I want you to try to be calm."

"Wait," said Sam. "So the baby's going to be born today?"

"Sir, your baby is going to be born in the next hour."

The baby was in footling breech position, meaning he was coming out feet first. Many hospitals feel this can be dangerous and do C-sections by policy. In my case, though, the baby was moving through the birth canal so quickly that there was apparently no time to waste. It was amazing to witness how fast medical personnel can move when they have to. We arrived at the hospital at approximately six in the morning, and a little before seven thirty, our son, Nathan Joseph Roth, was placed screaming on my chest.

When they took him in to be cleaned up and weighed, Sam said, bewildered, "Whose baby is that crying?"

"Ours!" I shouted. "He's right in the next room."

"Oh."

I don't know why I thought to immediately ask, "What's the weight?"

Sam went to find out. "He's a little over four and a half pounds," he told me proudly.

"What?" I said. "He shouldn't be that tiny. He's only four weeks early."

Nathan was indeed what is termed small for gestational age. The nurses noticed that his blood sugar was dropping. The neonatologists were concerned and they admitted him to the NICU.

Although I was recovering from my C-section, I insisted on going to Nathan's floor multiple times a day to hold and feed him. Since I still had a cold, I wore a surgical mask over my face to protect him from infection. Then it was time for me to be discharged, but they were still running tests on Nathan. I'd be going home without my baby.

The weight of the last year just sank me. I packed up my hospital room in slow motion while Sam went downstairs to get the car. I let a new mom and her baby, tucked snugly into an infant car seat, get into the elevator ahead of me so I wouldn't have to ride with them. When the next car arrived, I stood in it alone. I bowed my head, and tears ran down my cheeks and onto the floor.

But then I looked up, because the elevator car was suddenly filled with my mother's scent. I knew it anywhere. I didn't have anything of Mom's with me, of course, so there was no logical explanation. I smiled through my tears. It was a miracle she could still provide comfort.

Rich, Bea, and Gretchen flew out, as we all thought Nathan's discharge would be imminent. But every day when I'd arrive at the hospital, they had a new reason why he couldn't come home. Five days into Nathan's NICU stay, one of the neonatologists cornered me in the waiting room, without Sam, and told me they were testing the baby for a variety of global syndromes. She was so busy drawing Nathan's endocrine system on the back of a freaking hospital napkin that at first, she failed to impart that many of these were fatal.

When I absorbed that information, I was hysterical. My legs collapsed under me, and I huddled in the corner and sobbed in full view of everyone there. On that day, my life had reached a new low. Would my suffering never end?

Gretchen was a wonderful source of support, and Sam's dad Rich and his girlfriend Bea were too at first. They had been planning to stay with us for a week, at which time my father would arrive to help out. But as we anxiously waited for the results of Nathan's final tests, Bea came to me and said she and Rich wanted to leave early. Her daughter's husband had won a free trip with work and wanted Bea to come back east to babysit.

It was hard, bordering on impossible, for me to admit that I was cracking and needed other people to hold the pieces together. Theoretically, I understood that for Bea, her own flesh-and-blood children and grandchildren would always come before my family. But my baby could be dying, and if he did, I thought I might want to go with him.

In our living room, I sat under an old afghan, my face temporarily stoic. "Are you kidding?" I said to my in-laws.

"Nathan's going to be fine," Rich said.

"Hopefully," I said. "But that's not the point. I can't believe you're even asking me this."

"Don't get upset, honey," Rich said.

"Don't get upset? How would you feel if you were always everyone's second, third, tenth priority?"

"We don't have to go," Bea said. "They can find another babysitter."

"No, you know what? Go. I don't care."

It probably sounded like bluster, but it wasn't. I wasn't a fan of guilting people into doing things they didn't want to do. The fact that them leaving was even on the table was devastating to me. I didn't see how forcing them to stay because "it was the right thing to do" would help anyone.

To their credit, I guess, Rich and Bea did not leave. Nathan was released from the NICU a few days later. In the end, there was nothing wrong with him other than a correctable birth defect and an underactive thyroid gland. He was eating like a champ (or like a Roth, as Sam said) and had gained nearly a pound in his first week of life. This, according to the NICU docs, was the best possible sign.

So we took him home bundled in a little blue sweater, hat, and blanket that my grandmother had knitted. My dad arrived, and he, Rich, Bea, and Gretchen helped us with baths, feedings, and laundry. As a low-birthweight preemie, Nathan had to eat all the time, so Rich and Bea generously gifted us a night nurse for a few weeks. In those early days, the extra sleep made all the difference in my mood.

Nathan left the hospital on his ninth day of life, one day too late to have a traditional Jewish bris. Although a local rabbi came by to bless him instead, I was disappointed. I just wanted my child to have a normal life, and already, things were not quite right.

We were kept busy by people from the Elmhurst Newcomers and Neighbors club dropping by with food. Word got out in the group that I'd had a preemie, and the innate Midwestern desire to help those in need kicked in immediately. It was the first time in my life that I was part of a real community, and I observed the phenomenon curiously, as if visiting an alien world. After a few weeks, the last of our family went back to the East Coast, and it was time for Sam, Nathan, and me to forge a new routine as a family of three.

I surprisingly settled into motherhood naturally. After Nathan's birth, I'd decided to leave DDB and run my writing and consulting business full time. However, my new role as an entrepreneur meant that I couldn't take a real maternity leave. My second and third books were being published that year, and I'd learned that though the manuscripts were in, my work was far from over. I carried Nathan around in a ring sling as I did media interviews over the phone, and I composed blog posts and op-eds for the *New York Times* while in the pediatrician's waiting room.

I cuddled him close to me and kissed him incessantly. He stared at me with enormous black eyes. "Yes, I am your mother, sir," I said. "I don't know what I'm doing yet, but I promise to figure it out. I won't let you down."

Other moms with new babies joined me for short walks in the still-frozen Chicago tundra. We pushed our infants in identical Snap-N-Go strollers, their little bodies invisible under the mound of blankets and carseat covers.

"My mother criticizes everything I do with Caden," one mom, Hilary, complained as we meandered through the park. "She has to comment on everything. It's like, who cares whether I swaddle in a blanket or a sleep sack?"

"She's probably just trying to help," I said.

"She needs to leave."

I grimaced. "You don't mean that."

"She's been obsessed with this baby since I got my first period," Hilary said. "And now she wants to be over all the time."

"But it's another perspective," I said. "An extra pair of hands. If you're worried about something, or even if Caden just did something cool, you know she'll appreciate it."

"I guess so."

The thing was, Hilary wasn't the anomaly. I was. I heard my mother's voice in my head. "You'll regret not having a mother for the rest of your life." Because she was right. I did regret it. Nathan and I didn't have a situation like Hilary and Caden, and we never would.

Listening to Hilary and my other friends with ever-present mothers, I began to grieve again. Objectively, my life *was* better without one particular Susan Golden in it. But no matter what I did, how hard I tried, no one would ever be dedicated to me the way my mother should have been. I mourned what I would never have in a mother and what Nathan and any future children would never have in a grandmother. The agony ripped through my veins; the resentment seeped from my pores.

As Nathan grew, healthy and strong and catching up to his peers size-wise within two months, I also began to suffer from paralyzing anxiety about his health. It was as if the moment when the neonatologist had told me he might not live was on replay. I stopped taking Nathan out in public for fear he would get sick. I stood by his crib for hours to make sure he was still breathing.

One weekend, some friends from the city trekked all the way out to Elmhurst with a lasagna. They were still on our porch when they mentioned their daughter Joy was sick. "They can't see the baby," I hissed to Sam.

"But they aren't sick. Joy is. She isn't with them."

"I know, but they could be carriers."

"Ally, they came all the way here."

"We can't, Sam. I'm sorry."

At the end of May, I was scheduled to travel to San Diego for a series of speaking engagements. But the trip meant leaving Nathan for four days. I canceled.

I thought I saw my mother everywhere I went. I didn't sleep and couldn't focus on my work. I counted the seconds until the next bad thing happened.

My therapist was alarmed by my symptoms. A new assessment revealed that I was suffering from post-traumatic stress disorder (PTSD), an illness that I associated with combat veterans but that was surprisingly common among mothers of premature babies. I restarted the antidepressant I'd taken in college and began a regimen of cognitive-behavioral therapy with the goal of changing certain negative patterns of thinking. As in, let's keep track of all the positive things and negative things that happened with Nathan over the course of the day. Which list is longer? The activities from my therapist were hands-on and pragmatic and appealed to the problem-solver in me.

The temperate, early June days appeased us with their promise of a heat-soaked, Midwestern summer, and gradually, I began to feel better.

Nathan surprised us every day. One dewy morning, he and I relaxed on the lawn in our backyard with a blanket and some toys. I placed him on his stomach for "tummy time," or exercises designed to strengthen a baby's head and neck muscles. Wearing a *Lost* onesie that was a gift from Liz, Nathan rolled immediately onto his back.

I clapped my hands in delight. "What a good boy! You aren't supposed to be able to do that for at least another month!"

He treated me to a gummy smile and turned his attention to rolling back onto his tummy. "Come on, sweet guy. You can do it!"

He would, too. Just in time for Daddy to come home and see it.

Despite our changed family circumstances, Sam and I leapt forward in our careers. I was starting to become well known in my field, and the consulting arm of my business took off as I landed large new clients like Microsoft and McDonald's. Sam received funding for his first National Institute of Health grant for a new form of stem cell research.

That fall, allowed to focus on my own emotional well-being for the first time in my life, I learned an appreciation for the simple things—like cheering at a Northwestern football game, barbecuing in the backyard with friends, and bouncing a laughing baby on my lap during a Mommy and Me music class. I relearned how to love. I saw qualities in myself that I hoped to pass on to my son—strength and resilience. In October, Sam, Nathan, and I participated in the American Foundation for Suicide Prevention's annual Chicago fundraising walk on behalf of Mom.

As we were strolling under the orange-and-red elm trees, I whispered a wish to Nathan, who was clapping his chubby hands at all the fanfare and squirming to get out and crawl: "I want you to be happy all your life, little love. It doesn't matter what else you accomplish or who you turn out to be, as long as you have that."

As we approached the year anniversary of my mother's death, I took training to become an AFSP survivor outreach volunteer. The role involved visiting the families and friends of those who had recently committed suicide. Listening to their stories, and offering support and resources. AFSP does not allow people to volunteer in this way until they are at least a year past their personal loss, and I understood why. By this time, I had started to remake myself. I wasn't so broken, and it wasn't so painful to speak about the tragedy of my mother's life and death. I could be relieved, without guilt, that she was no longer suffering and that I was at last free to live my own life.

And then, at the beginning of November, Rich and Bea came out from New York for a visit. The five of us got up early on Sunday the third and drove to Montrose Beach on the north side of Chicago, not far from Northwestern University. I held the urn containing my mother's cremated remains gingerly in my lap while Sam drove.

We parked in the lot of the deserted beach and walked to the water's edge, our only company a few squawking gulls. Lake Michigan is stunning, but it doesn't quite make sense to native East Coasters.

The waves pound against the sandy shore, and because you can't see through to the other side, it looks like the ocean. But the salt in the air is missing, and if you go underwater, you come up with eyes that are bright and clear.

We each said a few words and recited the Jewish prayer of mourning. I didn't cry. I didn't want to, and wouldn't berate myself for that. The person I was had allowed me to survive. I couldn't be anyone else.

I closed my eyes and saw Mom at age thirty-three, thin and pretty and smart and funny. I saw her on the beach sipping a can of Tab, in love with her husband and little daughter. I thought about how devastating it must have been for her to create the life she'd always wanted as a lonely child, and then watch as year by year it slipped further away. I'd realized how difficult it was to be a mother the moment my son was born, and I was hopelessly in love with and afraid for him. How terrible it must have been for Mom to have to do everything that parents do, feel everything that parents feel, in her thunderstorm of a world.

I let the ashes go. The early-morning winter wind whipped around us so ferociously that the remains scattered in all directions and not just over the water as intended. Some flew into my face and hair, pieces of Mom burrowing themselves into my body, her cells joined with mine just as they had been from the very beginning. And then my tiny son reached his hand up to me, and we marched off the beach in the direction of home.

FURTHER READING AND SUPPORT

Websites

- American Association of Suicidology (suicidology.org)
- American Foundation for Suicide Prevention (afsp.org)
- American Psychiatric Association (psychiatry.org)
- American Psychological Association (apa.org)
- Borderline Personality Disorder Informational Site (bpdcentral.com)
- Borderline Personality Disorder Online Support Network (bpdfamily.com)
- Foundation for Excellence in Mental Health Care (mentalhealthexcellence.org)
- National Alliance on Mental Illness (nami.org)
- National Education Alliance for Borderline Personality Disorder (borderlinepersonalitydisorder.com)
- National Institute of Mental Health (nimh.nih.gov)
- National Suicide Prevention Resource Center (sprc.org)
- Psychology Today (psychologytoday.com)

Books

- *All the Things We Never Knew* by Sheila Hamilton

- *The Buddha and the Borderline* by Kiera Van Gelder
- *Call Me Tuesday* by Leigh Byrne
- *Darkness Visible* by William Styron
- *The Family Guide to Borderline Personality Disorder* by Alan Fruzzetti
- *History of a Suicide* by Jill Bialosky
- *I Hate You, Don't Leave Me* by Jerold Kreisman and Hal Straus
- *Motherless Daughters* by Hope Edelman
- *No Time to Say Goodbye* by Carla Fine
- *Out Came the Sun* by Mariel Hemingway
- *Stop Walking on Eggshells* by Randi Kreger and Paul Mason
- *Toxic Parents* by Susan Forward

ABOUT THE AUTHOR

Ally Golden was born in Michigan in 1976. She was raised in the suburbs of Washington, DC and graduated from Northwestern University in Evanston, IL. Ally is a freelance writer and consultant whose work has appeared in publications including *the Wall Street Journal, the New York Times, Fast Company,* and *the Atlantic.* Enjoying kickboxing, singing, traveling, and reading/watching science fiction, Ally lives in Chicago with her husband and two children and is a passionate advocate for families suffering from a loved one's mental illness.

Made in the USA
Lexington, KY
06 April 2017